Moonfixer

Earl at the peak of his basketball career, with the Syracuse Nationals.
(Courtesy of NBA Photos/Getty Images)

Moonfixer

The Basketball Journey of Earl Lloyd

Earl Lloyd *and* Sean Kirst

With a Foreword by Dave Bing

Syracuse University Press

Syracuse, New York 13244-5290

First Edition 2010

10 11 12 13 14 15 6 5 4 3 2 1

∞ The paper used in this publication meets the minimum requirements of the American National Standard for Information Sciences—Permanence of Paper for Printed Library Materials, ANSI Z39.48-1992.

For a listing of books published and distributed by Syracuse University Press, visit our Web site at SyracuseUniversityPress.syr.edu.

ISBN: 978-0-8156-0946-9

Library of Congress Cataloging-in-Publication Data

Lloyd, Earl, 1928–

Moonfixer : the basketball journey of Earl Lloyd / Earl Lloyd and Sean Kirst.

p. cm.

Includes index.

ISBN 978-0-8156-0946-9 (cloth : alk. paper)

1. Lloyd, Earl, 1928– 2. African American basketball players—Biography.
3. Syracuse Nationals (Basketball team) 4. Detroit Pistons (Basketball team)
I. Kirst, Sean Peter. II. Title.

GV884.L59A3 2009

796.323092—dc22

[B] 2009042203

Manufactured in the United States of America

I dedicate this book to my parents, Theodore and Daisy Lloyd; my brothers, Ernest and Ted; my sons, Kenneth, Kevin, and David; my grandchildren; and to the love of my life, my beautiful bride, Charlita. Without them, none of this would have been remotely possible.

—Earl Lloyd

Earl Lloyd, born into segregation in 1928, attended Parker-Gray High School in Alexandria, Virginia, before graduating from West Virginia State College. He was drafted by the Washington Capitols of the National Basketball Association and played in the league for eight seasons, most of them in Syracuse. He was the first African American to compete in an NBA game, and he also broke down long-standing barriers as an NBA coach, as a scout, and as an executive with the Dodge division of Chrysler. He was deeply involved in programs to benefit city youth in Detroit. He eventually retired from a position with the Bing Group, operated by Dave Bing, one of Lloyd's former players and a close friend. Lloyd has received many honors in recent years, including his 2003 enshrinement in the Naismith Memorial Basketball Hall of Fame.

Sean Kirst is a columnist for the *Post-Standard*, the daily newspaper in Syracuse, New York. In thirty-five years as a working journalist, a career that began when he was fourteen, he has been involved in covering such stories as the fate of the evacuated Love Canal neighborhood in Niagara Falls, the aftermath of the bombing of Pan Am Flight 103 over Lockerbie in Scotland, and the everyday struggles of working families across Upstate New York. Kirst has received many national honors for his work, including the 2008 Ernie Pyle Award for human interest writing, given annually by the Scripps-Howard Foundation to the one newspaper writer who most exemplifies the ethic of the famed World War II correspondent. Kirst, also the author of *The Ashes of Lou Gehrig, and Other Baseball Essays,* lives in Syracuse with his wife, Nora, and their three children.

Contents

Illustrations

Foreword

Mayor Dave Bing

A superb basketball career at Syracuse University and in the National Basketball Association carried Dave Bing into the Naismith Memorial Basketball Hall of Fame. He spent most of his NBA career with the Detroit Pistons. After retiring from the game in 1978, he became a prominent businessman and civic leader in Detroit. In 2009, responding to political and financial turmoil in the city, Bing was elected to serve as Detroit's sixty-second mayor.

Earl Lloyd is my close friend today, but I first heard of him when I was a young man. I grew up in Washington, D.C., and he was raised right across the bridge, in Alexandria.

As a kid, growing up and watching the NBA, I knew he was the first African American to play in the league. It was obvious, and those of us who followed basketball talked about it. I didn't get to know Earl until I was playing for Syracuse University. I knew he'd played in Syracuse, in the NBA, because I was pretty friendly with Dolph Schayes and some of the other Nats who'd been his teammates. As I got toward the end of my college career, Earl was a scout for the Pistons, and that's how we really met; Detroit had a first-round choice in the draft, and I was the guy he wanted the team to take. We formed a good relationship back then, and once I got to Detroit he was kind of a big brother.

It was a tough situation. Cazzie Russell was also in the draft that year, and he had played his college ball just down the road at Ann Arbor, and many people around Detroit were very disappointed when the Knicks took Cazzie and Detroit got me instead. Earl was always strong in my corner: "We got Dave," he kept saying, "and you guys will realize we got the best player." He was always that way, both in the press and as a voice behind the scenes. He was always encouraging me and telling me not to get down.

Training camp that year was difficult. It was my first training camp, and I didn't know what to expect. A big part of my game was being quick, and we played a lot of half court in practice. The Pistons had a couple of big veterans at guard, Eddie Miles and Tommy Van Arsdale, and when you're playing half court against guys that size, your quickness and speed don't help very much. They outweighed me by thirty, forty pounds. That held me down until we played full court, and they couldn't keep up. I had the quickness, the ability to penetrate, and it changed everything about how our team approached the game. Even then, it wasn't easy at first. I liked to pass the ball, too, and a lot of my teammates didn't know how to play with me. They didn't know what to expect, especially some of the big guys.

Through all of this, Earl was supportive. As a rookie, Dave DeBusschere was my head coach. He was a young guy in his twenties, and he wasn't really in a position to make many changes. Most of the guys on the team expected Cazzie to be there, and didn't know what to make of me. Even though I played well in camp and in the exhibition season, Dave wasn't ready to make the big change. He was comfortable with Eddie, and comfortable with Van Arsdale. I remember our first game was against Cincinnati, which had Oscar Robertson, a great player. I had always marveled at him but never had the chance to play against him. In the locker room, when Dave was telling us who would start, I thought for sure he would call my name. When he didn't, I was deflated. Once I got into the game, I was so in awe of Oscar, I went scoreless for the first time in my career. I think I shot 0 for 6 from the floor, and the press was already wondering if I was a flash in the pan. It took about ten games before I was inserted into the starting lineup, and then things went very well.

All these years later, I remember how Earl was there for me, and what he'd done for all of us in the years before that. When I got to Detroit, I think we had three white players on the team. The league had started to become predominately African American. We didn't have the same problems as Earl and the others who came in before us. They caught the brunt of the racism, and made it easier for us. By the time I got to the NBA, there was a real movement for change in the country. I always had conversations about those changes with Earl, and I think those of us coming in at the time understood what those earlier guys had endured.

Later on, Earl would become my coach, a very good coach, a player's coach. He just had that kind of personality that no matter what decision he made, you agreed, because he was such a good person. You knew he was doing what he thought was the right thing. You never spoke against him. He understood the game from every perspective, and he was "old school" in the sense that he wanted you to fit in with everyone else, even if you were the best player on the team. If you didn't do what was expected, he would never embarrass you; he would quietly take you aside.

What makes our relationship special is that it only began with basketball; it didn't end there. I joke with Earl that he's one of the few people who ought to get four or five pensions. He played and coached for years in the NBA, and he spent years working with Chrysler, and he did good work with the police department in Detroit. I reached out to him long after I left the Pistons. My life had gotten pretty complex. I was trying to run a business and do all the things I was asked to do in the community, and there wasn't time enough to do everything, and I needed someone I could trust to go out and represent me. And there was Earl, already a pillar in the community. We had a long and very good professional relationship, and he did everything I could have asked him to do.

Most important, he put in countless hours talking to young people in Detroit. I think they touched a soft place in his heart. He saw these generations that came after him, young people who were taking some things for granted and didn't always appreciate the struggles his generation went through, and he talked to them about it. He understood what it took for people in his era to succeed, with everything going against them. I think it always bothered him when these later generations assumed they had success only because of what they had done themselves, and not because someone else was there to lay the groundwork. Earl understood who laid the groundwork for him. With him, it's always about those who came before.

I don't think Earl dislikes anyone, and anyone who's ever been around him cannot dislike the guy. He's the nicest guy you'd ever want to meet, and he's always got a story; he's got a talent for always being able to relate a story to what you're going through. I think because of those qualities, because he's humble and comes across as such a nice guy, that it's easy to forget just what he accomplished. What he did was exceedingly important. There's no doubt about it. If he had been a different kind of personality, it would have been very difficult for the black players who came after him to succeed or be accepted. He was always a gentleman, never flamboyant, never walking around with a chip on his shoulder, even if he deserved to feel that way. He dealt with all these negative things young players today would never even believe. Because of the way he carried himself, he opened doors for the rest of us. I'm glad our league office constantly brings him back to talk to our rookies, because he brings the knowledge these kids need.

So many of our young people today don't understand our history. They just don't know. Earl gives them that history. He wasn't always a prolific scorer or an all-star player. Many of these kids never heard of him. But no player should matter more to them. I don't think he's ever been jealous of the kind of money or lifestyle these young men command now. Earl never made a lot of money, but he paved the way for the big contracts today because of what he did and endured. He went through all of it for today's players. It's a connection they have to understand. To know who you are today, and what you need to do, you have to know what it was like throughout the history of this country, back to slavery. A lot of these kids don't know what it was like. They make assumptions that because they can go anywhere and live where they want to live, that it must have always been that way. Taking them back, making them realize things weren't always like this, educating them about the struggle: you've got to have somebody to connect the players of today with the players of yesterday, and Earl's the best person to do it, a living example.

There is another thing these kids need to learn. I can tell you a lot of stories about the way Earl handles success, but what I vividly remember is how he handled life when things went wrong. When he was fired as our coach, I was devastated and hurt. We'd had a constant coaching turnover, and now we had lost a guy we really respected and loved, a guy trying to do all the right things when he just didn't have the talent on the roster to win games. When the Pistons let him go, it caught us by surprise, because he wasn't just a coach but a dear friend. That was a double whammy. But he accepted his firing with a lot of class. He could have blasted the organization, but he didn't. He walked away with dignity. That's how he is.

Over the years, I've gotten to know his family—his wife, his kids, his grandkids. Our families know each other pretty well. It's a throwback to when there wasn't a lot of fanfare or a lot of money in basketball; the real lasting value came through your relationships. It was a blessing, and part of our friendship is built on my appreciation for what Earl endured.

My mother and father are from South Carolina. When I was leaving high school, I had more than two hundred scholarship offers around

1. Dave Bing in 2008, not long before he was elected mayor of Detroit, during a visit to Syracuse to raise money for scholarships for children of the city. Bing and Earl share a friendship that goes back to Bing's playing days at Syracuse University. (Photo by Stephen D. Cannerelli, courtesy of the *Post-Standard*)

the country. The one thing I knew was that I wasn't going to a southern school. I'd go south with my parents, and we couldn't get a drink or eat in certain places. D.C., by then, wasn't so bad. Even so, from kindergarten through tenth grade, I had never gone to school with someone who didn't look like me.

All of those factors played a role in why I decided to go to Syracuse. Most people thought it was nuts, that I'd made a mistake. Syracuse was a big school without many African American students. I could go days without seeing someone who looked like me. But that's what made me the person I am today. In D.C., I saw one thing, and in Syracuse I saw something that was completely different. It taught me to deal with all kinds of people, and I made a hell of a lot of friends there. I think what it comes down to is having respect for your fellow man, more than anything. Doesn't matter how much money you have, or how much education. Doesn't matter what color you are. All that matters in the end is that you're a good human being and that you believe in having respect for one another.

Always, to me, that's what Earl represents.

Preface

Earl Lloyd and Syracuse

Sean Kirst

You'd have a hard time finding any reminder in Syracuse of what Earl Lloyd accomplished during his time in that Upstate city in New York. No school, street, or playground carries his name, even though Lloyd spent most of his playing career in the National Basketball Association with the old Syracuse Nationals, who later moved to Philadelphia and became the '76ers. Lloyd joined the Nats for the 1952–53 season, after he was honorably discharged from the army, and spent six seasons with the team before he was traded to Detroit. Even during his peak years, little was made of his groundbreaking status in basketball history. Despite the attention paid to racial pioneers in other sports, reporters in the 1950s rarely wrote or spoke about Lloyd's extraordinary role in the game, an oversight that would only begin to be remedied in 2003, when Lloyd was inducted into the Naismith Memorial Basketball Hall of Fame.

Yet his status can be seen as increasingly monumental, particularly when set alongside the role basketball plays in black America. On Halloween night, 1950, as a member of the Washington Capitols, Lloyd became the first African American to play in an NBA game when he took the court in Rochester against the Royals, whose franchise survives as the Sacramento Kings. As you'll learn in this book, Lloyd prefers to downplay his own significance. He'll tell you the real cultural groundbreakers for black America within the realm of sports were Joe Louis, the heavyweight champion boxer, and Jackie Robinson, who in 1947—as a member of the Brooklyn Dodgers—shattered longtime racial barriers in Major League Baseball.

Lloyd's admirers have a different view. Al Attles, a former NBA player and coach who became an executive with the Golden State Warriors, may have put it best when he said that what Lloyd did "softened the bed for the rest of us."

Ask Lloyd, and he'll remind you that he was one of four blacks to play at least a few NBA games in the 1950–51 season, and that one of those contemporaries, Chuck Cooper, was taken much earlier in the league's annual draft. Cooper was picked by the Boston Celtics in the second round, while Lloyd went in the ninth. Lloyd also maintains that basketball had already gone through a more gradual integration process, which offered him a gentler entry than the harsh and threatening landscape that Robinson had to navigate in Major League Baseball.

Unlike baseball, Lloyd says, most professional basketball players had a college education, which gave them at least some basis for contemplating the benefits of tolerance. And by 1950 many white pros in the NBA had already competed at some point in their careers against teams with one or two players of color.

The best way to judge the importance of Lloyd's role may be to look at it through the prism of Syracuse, a then prosperous Upstate New York industrial city—its population in 1950 was at an all-time peak of 220,000—that had a wildly erratic history involving blacks and elite athletics. Indeed, you can argue that Lloyd's major accomplishment in Syracuse was to shatter an unspoken national ban that began in the same city.

Most of us are familiar with the tale of a legendary meeting between Branch Rickey and Jackie Robinson, just before Robinson signed a contract to play for the Dodgers. Rickey was president of the Brooklyn team and ran its baseball operations. He was the guy who made the decision to crack baseball's color line, but he also believed he needed a player strong enough to hold down the natural response of personal fury to vitriolic racism.

Rickey understood that any kind of explosion or violence on the part of the first black in the Major Leagues—no matter how justified—would reinforce the ugliest stereotypes and fears throughout America, thus setting back efforts not only to integrate baseball but to transform fundamental aspects of life in this nation. In 1947, across the United States, most black men and women could not aspire to be police officers or firefighters or teachers or journalists (at least not for mainstream "white" newspapers). The doors to almost any meaningful job were open only to whites. Robinson's importance, then, would extend far beyond sports, a reality that he and Rickey clearly understood. With all of that at stake, the story goes, Rickey took Robinson into his office and put him to the test.

With Robinson seated in a chair, Rickey began walking back and forth, saying every vile thing that he could conjure up about Robinson's color, about his family, about his manhood. Rickey poured it on with such venom that Robinson struggled to control his rage, although he managed to force down that fury and stay calm.

Finally, Rickey finished. Face taut, the young man in the office said nothing, and the Dodgers executive knew he had made the right choice. Robinson would break into the International League in 1946 with Montreal, where his treatment from the old Syracuse Chiefs would be particularly onerous. But the critical issue is that Robinson resisted the urge to lash back, despite the beanballs and vile insults that followed him from his debut in the International League through his first few seasons with Brooklyn.

While baseball was being reluctantly forced to move forward by Robinson and Rickey, an incident in Syracuse—less than two months before Robinson's debut with the Dodgers—would set back efforts to make similar changes in professional basketball. In the days before the NBA, there were two major professional basketball leagues. Teams from many of the larger cities competed in the old Basketball Association of America (BAA), which considered itself the true major league. The rival National Basketball League included franchises in such cities as Syracuse and Oshkosh— teams whose owners hardly conceded superiority to the other league. In its underdog role, the NBL was ready to take chances. As early as 1942 some team executives were signing black players, and the dominant black player in the league—if not the best player in the game, period—would turn out to be William "Pop" Gates.

In 1946 Leo Ferris, then an administrator with a short-lived NBL club in Buffalo, signed Gates to a contract. The team would soon relocate to Moline, Illinois, where the franchise was called the Tri-Cities Blackhawks. Gates, a skilled forward, was a veteran of some of the great all-black teams known as the Renaissance Five, or the New York Rens. He was a tenacious scorer who drew the attention of the league's most aggressive defenders; those skills would eventually lift him into the Hall of Fame.

If Gates ever received the same turn-the-other-cheek speech as Robinson, he didn't talk about it. The dynamics of basketball are profoundly different from baseball. It is a sport played in close proximity, in a venue where it becomes almost impossible not to hit back. That point was made explosively clear on February 24, 1947, when Tri-Cities visited Syracuse for a key game while both teams were clawing for a playoff spot. The game was played in the old Jefferson Street Armory, the Nats' home at the time, and the team asked John "Chick" Meehan, a well-loved hometown star, to take his best shot at guarding Gates.

Meehan was a tough and physical player who had no fear of making contact. With five minutes left in the game, the two men went after a loose ball. Meehan went down, pushed by Gates, who later said the shove was in retaliation for a relentless hammering throughout the game. Furious, Meehan climbed to his feet and said, "What the hell?" An equally furious Gates floored him with a punch.

The place erupted. Hundreds of fans stormed onto the court and headed straight toward Gates. National Guardsmen from the armory rushed out to form a cordon around him, and the game was stopped with Syracuse leading, 53-47. That explosion of rage would underline the meaning of Rickey's warnings to Robinson. Whether Gates was right or wrong didn't matter; what mattered was the reaction of the men who ran the league. "Race was the only explanation for why so many fans had jumped into the melee," author John Christgau wrote in his book *Tricksters in the Madhouse,* which discusses the racial equation in basketball in the 1940s. The *Syracuse Post-Standard* described the incident as a potential "race riot" in an article the next day. While Gates would later apologize to Meehan—and both men always said the altercation had nothing to do with color—worried owners took the fight in Syracuse as good reason to shy away from integration.

There would be no black players on any roster when the BAA and NBL merged into the NBA for the 1949–50 season. Years later, in Gates's obituary, the *New York Times* cited the fight in Syracuse as the reason the new league closed the door on blacks, thus moving the NBA in the opposite direction of baseball, which by that time was erasing its color line.

Into this situation, in 1950, walked Earl Lloyd, a six-foot-five, 220-pound power forward. Drafted by Washington, he would play the majority of his NBA games at the War Memorial auditorium in Syracuse, a few blocks away from the place where Gates had to be protected from the crowd.

Certainly, as Lloyd will readily tell you, Robinson's trials in Brooklyn were more famous and more symbolically important on a national level. Yet Lloyd, for his part, represents the quiet and important move toward equality in countless smaller communities. Despite his humility at his own accomplishments, the pressures and challenges for Lloyd were similar to the ones symbolized by Robinson: how Lloyd carried himself, and the impressions that he made, would have implications for all the black players who followed him.

He was born April 3, 1928, in Alexandria, Virginia, in the shadow of Washington, D.C. From infancy into his early years as a professional basketball player, Lloyd lived under the yoke of legal segregation, or "Jim Crow." As he is quick to recall, he did not have anything akin to a real conversation with a white man or woman until he went to his first training camp for the NBA.

Lloyd was the third and youngest son of Theodore and Daisy Lloyd. His father shoveled coal. His mother was a homemaker who earned a few extra dollars by cleaning the homes of white families; she also worked for a time in a naval torpedo station during World War II. As Lloyd explains in this book, his awakening about racial injustice happened gradually throughout his childhood, until it came home fully in his teenage years. His parents routinely warned him about where he could and couldn't go. They laid out the potential results if he tried to rebel against riding in the back of the bus or using the "Colored only" water fountain.

The cruelties of the time were manifest at Parker-Gray High School in Alexandria. Lloyd was a star in three sports: baseball, basketball, and football. Yet his school teams wore tattered uniforms and had no decent facilities, in stark contrast to the nearby, all-white, George Washington High. Lloyd would often travel into Washington on weekends to watch the Washington Bears, an all-black team consisting of many of the great players from the New York Rens. Lloyd's favorite player was Sonny Woods, a "smooth-as-silk backcourtman who could really play." If Lloyd had any professional aspirations, it was a dream of playing for an all-black outfit like the Rens.

He graduated from high school in 1946, the year Robinson signed a contract with Brooklyn and went to play with the Montreal Royals. As for Lloyd, he accepted a scholarship at West Virginia State College—now a university—an all-black school that was also the alma mater of the high school coach Lloyd revered, Louis Johnson.

Those college years remain especially dear to Lloyd. On campus, for the first time, he was spared the racial degradation and humiliation that had been a daily part of life in Virginia. His schoolmates called him "Moonfixer," a nickname, shortened to "Moon," that he hears to this day from old friends. He reveled in both the social and the academic elements of college, and he was intensely aware that his parents and teachers had sacrificed for years to get him there. He got the opportunity to show his appreciation on the basketball court.

In a segregated nation, West Virginia State was a black national power throughout Lloyd's years with the team. In his sophomore season of 1947–48, the school went 23-0, won the Colored Intercollegiate Athletic Association (CIAA) Championship, and was unofficially acclaimed as the nation's black collegiate champion. The school paper, the *Yellow Jacket*, reported on rumors that the all-white National Invitation Tournament (NIT) might offer a first-ever berth to a black college. It didn't happen; West Virginia State had to settle for a barnstorming tour on the West Coast, in which the school played some of the leading "white" colleges in California.

By the time Lloyd graduated, he had become an annual choice for the All-CIAA team. Although exact statistics from those seasons are difficult to find, old copies of the West Virginia State student newspaper indicate he averaged anywhere from fifteen to seventeen points a game.

Even then, Lloyd was not thinking about a career in mainstream pro basketball. When he was a senior, the Harlem Globetrotters gave him the chance to accompany the team on a quick tour; club management assumed that any top African American college ballplayer would inevitably choose to sign a contract with one of the few basketball operations available to blacks. The NBA, following the brawl in Syracuse, remained all-white. That explains why Lloyd was so startled in the spring of 1950 when he learned he'd been selected in the ninth round of the NBA draft by the Capitols.

Later that year, in front of 2,184 spectators on a Halloween night at the Edgerton Park Sports Arena in Rochester, Lloyd became the first black player to take part in an NBA game. Three other blacks—Cooper, Nat "Sweetwater" Clifton, and Hank DeZonie—would also participate in the league that season. But Lloyd was hardly the focus of attention in Rochester, where the Royals had won 51 of 68 games in their first season in the league. Their lineup included such eventual Hall of Famers as Bobby Davies, Bobby Wanzer, Red Holzman, and Arnie Risen. Local sportswriters were mainly interested in a stream of quotes from Bones McKinney, Washington's head coach, described as a "good showman and a great competitor" by George Beahon of the *Rochester Democrat & Chronicle* in a story on the morning of the opening game.

Deeper in the piece, as Beahon wound up an overview of Washington, he made reference to "Earl Lloyd, 6-6, Negro from W. Virginia State. Boston and New York are the only other teams in the NBA carrying Negro players this season, an innovation in the circuit."

That was about the extent of the local attention paid to Lloyd's debut, a far cry from the intense focus when Robinson broke in with the Dodgers. Yet Lloyd's debut was symbolic of a fast and sweeping change that would transform basketball more profoundly than any American sport. By 2009, only about 10 percent of the players in Major League baseball were African American, while black players held about 80 percent of the positions on NBA rosters.

No one sensed that coming in 1950, on a late October night in Rochester, where league president Maurice Podoloff ceremonially tossed up the ball for the first tip. The Royals won, 78-70. Lloyd had 6 points, 10 rebounds, and 5 assists. He would total 43 points and 47 rebounds in 7 games with the Capitols before he took a leave of absence to answer a draft notice from the U.S. Army.

While he was gone, the Capitols collapsed. Their players were made available in a special draft. The rights to Earl Lloyd were claimed by Syracuse.

His prime NBA years, then, would be spent in a city in Upstate New York with a spectacularly erratic history of dealing with race and athletics. Although Syracuse was considered one of the hotbeds of abolitionist sentiment before the Civil War, its everyday record on racial progress was more checkered. In 1889, while an infamous "gentleman's agreement" was forcing black players to leave professional baseball, Moses Fleetwood Walker was still catching for the Syracuse Stars of the old International League. He would remain the last black to play on that level in a "white" baseball league until Robinson joined the Montreal Royals, fifty-seven years later.

Walker ran into plenty of abuse around the league—with some of it coming from his own teammates, including pitchers who didn't want to throw the ball to a black catcher. He was released after that 1889 campaign. Two years later, still in Syracuse, Walker was walking across the city on what was described as a "baseball errand" when he was confronted by some white men in the street. Walker said they demanded to know why he was in their neighborhood, then insulted him, threw stones at him, and attacked. In the ensuing brawl, Walker stabbed a white man to death, setting up a murder trial that captured national attention.

Members of the black community in Syracuse could not sit in the courtroom; they had to wait in a crowd outside, while events were relayed to them by word of mouth. As the trial progressed, public opinion clearly grew to support Walker, who often sat in court with his small child on his lap, and who described under oath how his assailant called him a "damn nigger."

Finally, jury chairman James Hill, a farmer, stood and read a verdict of "not guilty." The courtroom exploded; cheering spectators rushed over to congratulate the Walkers. One newspaper account said that Judge George Kennedy pounded his gavel so hard in trying to regain order that the top of the gavel flew completely off.

As the twentieth century commenced, Syracuse evolved or stagnated on questions of racial equity in much the same way as other large northern industrial cities. Blacks could hold few meaningful jobs and were tacitly barred from many public clubs, taverns, and restaurants. The black community in Syracuse was essentially cordoned off within a neighborhood known as the Fifteenth Ward, where blacks lived alongside the city's Jews, who at the time were ostracized in much the same way.

In 1936 Wilmeth Sidat-Singh—a talented black basketball player from Harlem—began to navigate a treacherous path in Syracuse. In high school Sidat-Singh had been an extraordinarily gifted athlete, excelling at every sport he tried. He arrived at Syracuse University with plans to be a doctor, like his Indian stepfather. But he also intended to play basketball, which turned out to be a more painful choice than he imagined.

Sidat-Singh was African American. His father, William Webb, died when he was a child. His mother moved to Harlem, where she married Samuel Sidat-Singh, an Indian doctor. Since many schools remained reluctant to play against a black athlete, Syracuse tried to pass Sidat-Singh off as a "Hindu"—a ruse that worked for a while, until it was revealed by Sam Lacy, the celebrated black journalist.

As expected, Sidat-Singh was a star in basketball, although that was not how he earned his greatest collegiate fame. In 1937 Roy Simmons Sr., a Syracuse assistant football coach, saw Sidat-Singh playing catch with a friend on campus and convinced the young man to come out for the team. The newcomer quickly became a sensation for the Orange, particularly after famed columnist Grantland Rice watched him throw three late touchdown passes to beat powerful Cornell University.

His football prowess was intertwined with public humiliation. Syracuse had scheduled a road game against the Terrapins of Maryland. Sidat-Singh's family had roots in Washington, and many of his relatives made plans to come and watch. He never appeared in the game. Maryland threatened to boycott if Syracuse put a black player on the field, and the school backed down. Marty Glickman, the renowned broadcaster who played halfback on that Syracuse team, would often say his biggest regret in life was that no player stood up to speak for Sidat-Singh—a situation all too similar to what remains one of the most hurtful memories for Earl Lloyd in Syracuse.

Sidat-Singh would also be prevented from playing basketball against Navy, for the same reasons, when Syracuse visited Annapolis. At school he rented a room in the Fifteenth Ward, because he could not live in the dorms with white classmates. He was chosen to play for a college football

all-star team that took on the champions of the National Football League—but was quietly missing when practices began. As for the NFL, its doors at the time remained closed to blacks. Sidat-Singh ended up playing basketball for both the New York Rens and the Washington Bears, two of the great all-black teams of the era, before he enlisted to be a pilot during World War II.

He was training with other members of the Tuskegee Airmen, the celebrated all-black flying unit, when he was killed in a training accident above Lake Michigan. The student-athlete who could not live in the same dorm as his roommates died in the service of his country. He had been a close friend and roommate of Pop Gates when they played together on the Rens. Decades later, as an old man, Gates would often say that if Sidat-Singh had come home from the war, he would almost certainly have earned a place in the Naismith Memorial Basketball Hall of Fame.

For his part, Jackie Robinson, in interviews throughout his baseball career, often recalled the harsh treatment he received in Syracuse, only six years before Lloyd began playing for the Nats. In April 1946 Robinson was a high-profile member of the Montreal Royals when he arrived in Syracuse for an International League series against the Chiefs, who had many players from the Deep South. Robinson later said that the Syracuse players relentlessly taunted him, and even threw a black cat onto the field. Different versions of the story say that incident happened when Syracuse played the Royals in Montreal, but there is no doubt that the Chiefs treated Robinson as harshly as he was treated by any club in the International League. Garton Del Savio, a Chief who knew and admired Robinson, recalled that several of his teammates had to be restrained from taking the field, wearing blackface, when they played Montreal.

Despite that ugliness, there were signs of progress in Syracuse. In the late 1940s Ben Schwartzwalder—the new coach of the Syracuse University football team—not only began recruiting black players for his squad but also mandated that blacks and whites live together in the dorms. Horace Morris, the first African American to play for Schwartzwalder, recalled going to the Syracuse train station in 1946, only to find Robinson sitting on one side of the lobby—while the rest of his Montreal teammates sat on the other side. Morris sat down with Robinson and quietly told him about life

2. Jackie Robinson at MacArthur Stadium in Syracuse, while with the Montreal Royals. In 1946 he endured harsh racial taunting in that ballpark. (Courtesy of William Fitzpatrick)

as one of the few blacks on campus. "Kid, I'm going to make it," Robinson told him, "and you're going to make it, too."

By the time Lloyd got to Syracuse in 1952, the Chiefs were already a year past signing their first "black" player—Vic Power, a dark-skinned first baseman who considered himself to be Puerto Rican, not a black American. Even so, Power had no choice except to live with the rest of the black community in the Fifteenth Ward. At Syracuse, Schwartzwalder used a black quarterback, Bernie Custis, although black athletes at the school quietly bristled about unwritten rules against interracial dating.

News accounts of Lloyd's signing by the Nats made no mention of any of that tumultuous history. Yet Lloyd became another historic personality within an extraordinary collection of basketball characters in Syracuse, whose franchise had a pivotal role in transforming the NBA into a true major league. The primary owner was Danny Biasone, a shrewd and intuitive bowling alley operator whose main worry was putting people in the seats. The general manager was Leo Ferris, whose fierce tactics in the bidding war between the old NBL and BAA led to the creation of the modern NBA. The players resented Ferris for his manner and his tight ways with a dollar, but he was also a racial groundbreaker in his own right: in Buffalo, while working for Ben Kerner, Ferris had signed the great Pop Gates to a contract.

It was Biasone, Ferris, and Emil Barboni, a scout with the Nats, who took an idea proposed unsuccessfully for the college game by Howard Hobson of Yale and molded it into the professional rule known as the twenty-four-second shot clock—the innovation that increased speed and scoring and probably saved the NBA by bringing fans back to the games. As for Lloyd, he carried a strong recommendation from Fred Scolari, a former teammate who had gone to Syracuse. Biasone and Ferris couldn't help but see the bargain in Lloyd's considerable skills. The Nats did not look to him for scoring but instead counted on him for defense and rebounding, often asking him to guard the high scorers on opposing teams.

Lloyd lived out that mission, year after year. He was routinely asked to hold down elite scorers from around the league. Within three years of signing with the Nats, he would become the first black starter on an NBA championship team; he played a key role as the Nats defeated the Fort

Wayne Pistons for the title in seven games. That 1954–55 season was also Lloyd's best season as a scorer. He averaged 10.2 points per game, about a point and a half better than his career average, as part of a balanced, aggressive team that loved to run the court. In fitting symmetry, six months after Lloyd's Nats won the title, Robinson enjoyed his only World Series Championship in baseball when the Dodgers finally beat the Yankees.

Even as Lloyd quietly battled for rebounds in Syracuse, then walked home to a boardinghouse in the all-black Fifteenth Ward, the racial dynamic in America was heading toward dramatic change. A brilliant young orator, Dr. Martin Luther King Jr., had just become pastor of the Dexter Avenue Baptist Church in Montgomery, Alabama. Malcolm X, motivated by the revelations that had changed his life in prison, had become a passionate spokesman for the Nation of Islam. And in May 1954 the Supreme Court of the United States rendered its landmark decision in *Brown v. The Board of Education of Topeka, Kansas,* a ruling that basically proclaimed that the segregated conditions under which Earl Lloyd and millions of others went to school had violated the spirit and principles of American law.

As Lloyd wound down his career as a player, the fabric of the nation was being quietly remade. He retired as a player in 1959, but he stayed on with the Detroit Pistons to be a scout and the first black assistant coach in the league. For a brief and frustrating time, he would serve as head coach of the Pistons, before Lloyd settled on a career outside of basketball, recruiting black employees for positions with the Dodge division of the Chrysler Corporation. At the time, Lloyd says, there were twenty-six regions within the Dodge division with "zero black employees." He often laughs about how the first regional manager he met, in Cleveland, Ohio, was named Jim Crow.

Throughout the 1970s and well into the 1980s, his pioneering role in basketball seemed essentially forgotten. It was not until the 1990s that sports historians began to appreciate Lloyd's importance in the game. That rediscovery led to the ultimate acknowledgment in 2003, when Lloyd was inducted into basketball's Hall of Fame.

As for Syracuse, like so many cities across the nation, it has both evolved racially and in some ways fallen back. The old Fifteenth Ward was destroyed by the construction of new interstates, a process that civic leaders cheerfully called "slum control." Displaced black families moved to other neighborhoods, primarily the city's South Side, triggering a new wave of white flight—and leaving many areas in a continuing state of de facto segregation. While Syracuse has a true black middle class—and the city schools remain fragile but remarkably diverse—the African American community suffers from high levels of poverty and violence. Every year too many young black men die on the streets, and high school graduation rates remain tragically low for teens from the black community.

Those realities, mirrored in large cities across the United States, are part of the reason that Lloyd decided to tell his story. For years he kept many of his reflections to himself. As a young man, he adopted a simple philosophy: Anger is like acid. Set it loose, and it destroys you. He saw it happen too many times to childhood friends, driven into a self-defeating rage by the suffocating nature of the times. Yet he also lived to see the election of President Barack Obama, a moment of euphoria that Lloyd— who often walked the streets of Washington, D.C., when it was a segregated town—puts to words in the concluding pages of this book.

At eighty-one he offers testimony to a catastrophic era that many Americans have yet to honestly confront—a time of government-sanctioned cruelty and abuse that destroyed countless families and continues to scar cascading generations. Fifty years after retiring as a player, he is finally receiving some of the recognition he deserves. Lloyd appreciates the warm feelings, but he remains intensely aware of all those individuals crushed by the system he escaped and the millions who continue to suffer from the fallout.

To honor him, he would tell you, means we must remember them.

A Note to Readers

Sean Kirst

In 1991 I became a sports columnist with the *Syracuse Post-Standard*. The job had its priorities, notably covering Syracuse University football and basketball, but one fringe benefit was a chance to satisfy my curiosity about the old Nationals of the National Basketball Association. I'd grown up in Upstate New York, and I knew some of the history surrounding the team. Three of the men involved with running the Nats—Danny Biasone, Leo Ferris, and Emil Barboni—were responsible for the twenty-four-second shot clock, the innovation that transformed the once-tedious, half-court style of the NBA into a high-scoring, madly popular major league. The shot clock suited the fast-breaking team built in Syracuse by Biasone and Ferris. Before that innovation, the Nats had been perennially frustrated bridesmaids, twice losing in the NBA finals in the early 1950s to the dynastic Minneapolis Lakers. In 1954–55, the first season with the clock, Syracuse finally won it all by defeating Fort Wayne for the title.

By the time I began writing my columns for the *Post-Standard*, the Nats had been gone for almost thirty years, and their importance was often overlooked in their own town. That was soon brought home to me in the most profound of ways. I knew of the shot clock, and its role in basketball history. What I did not know was the extraordinary story of Earl Lloyd, which I began to appreciate only while digging through old files. Earl was a power forward on the 1955 NBA champions. He was also African American, and a few hours in the library at the *Post-Standard* brought me to a startling truth: In 1950 Earl became the first black American to officially set foot in an NBA game. He would then break ground as the first black starter on a championship team, the first black assistant coach in the NBA, and one of the league's earliest black head coaches. Symbolically and specifically, Earl was clearly among the most important players in the history of the game.

Even so, his significance was all but forgotten in the city where he spent most of his playing career, for reasons I only gradually began to understand. While Major League Baseball was utterly white before the arrival of Jackie Robinson in 1947, a few blacks had played in the 1940s in the old National Basketball League, which would merge—with the old Basketball Association of America—into what became the NBA. As basketball historian Bill Himmelman explained to me, such great black teams as the Harlem Globetrotters and the New York Rens had performed admirably at the old world championship competition in the 1930s and early 1940s in Chicago. The idea of integrating professional basketball was simply not as much of a jolt to white America as the notion of a black man in a Brooklyn Dodgers uniform. Earl was one of several blacks to cross the NBA threshold in 1950, and he was not the first African American to be drafted; as he will tell you, with emphasis, the fact that he was the first black to play in an NBA game was in many ways a function of the calendar. It could have just as easily been Chuck Cooper or Nat "Sweetwater" Clifton.

None of those details ought to detract from the enormity of his achievement, which grows in stature even as Earl moves into his eighties. Basketball has turned into an almost spiritual pastime within black America. For many young men and women, it is a statement of identity, as much a performance art as it is a sport. It came to be that way only because Earl and his contemporaries broke down those early walls. In 1992, during my first interview with Earl, I found him to be a thoughtful and profoundly self-effacing guy. He played down his own significance, heaped praise on his old Syracuse teammates, and told me repeatedly—as he does to this day—that he "was no Jackie Robinson." It is a point many of us would dispute.

Over the years, through many conversations with Earl, quiet truths about his character gradually emerged. I came to understand why his humility, sense of humor, and relentless humanity left lasting impressions on just about everyone he met. In Syracuse, for instance, he'd grown to be a close friend of Don "Peewee" Caldwell, a postal worker who also lived in the old Fifteenth Ward, the city neighborhood in which blacks in the 1950s were essentially confined. The two men were neighbors; the Caldwell home was near the boardinghouse where Earl stayed. What stands out for Caldwell is how Earl never considered himself to be anyone special; even during the time when Earl was a starter on an NBA championship team, they would often sit on Caldwell's porch, discussing sports or politics, before wandering into local jazz clubs to listen to fine musicians.

That impression was shared by some of the greatest figures in the game. During Earl's first weeks of training camp in 1950, when he was a rookie with the Washington Capitols, he'd often catch a ride to practice with Bill Sharman, one of his new teammates. Earl was black, Sharman white, and Earl never forgot the power of that gesture in a segregated America. Sharman, who went on to great fame as both a player and a coach, maintains that the daily ritual was a pleasure. "Earl was just a lovely, lovely person," he says. "In all the years I've known him, I don't think I've ever heard him have a harsh word for anyone."

That deep well of kindness and civility never softened the memories of a lifetime's worth of pain. As a child, Earl endured the full humiliation and cruelty of the system of legal segregation known as "Jim Crow," and he learned how to internalize a quiet, controlled anger. He used that fury as motivation, and rarely allowed any flash of it to show in public. Earl chose to contain the hurt, releasing it only in the occasional piercing observation.

As the decades rolled by and Earl became a father and grandfather, he grew increasingly aware of a need to share his reflections. By the late 1990s he was telling me he wanted to write a book, and he said he'd let me know when the right moment arrived. His family, he said, was urging him to get it done. Over the next few years he'd occasionally mention the idea, particularly after he was enshrined in 2003 in the Naismith Memorial Basketball Hall of Fame. At the time he said he wasn't quite ready to get started. In 2006 Earl said to me, "Once the New Year starts, let's go."

Since then, we've done dozens of interviews, often two or three a week. I visited Earl at his retirement home in Tennessee and accompanied him to a reunion at West Virginia State, the academic sanctuary that changed his life. Before long we had a towering pile of transcripts and notes, which underlines the most extraordinary aspect of the book that you're about to read: The ultimate statement on Earl's character is related as much to what stayed out of this book as what stayed in. It is a relatively fast read, and much of what we covered in our conversations did not make the final cut. Earl knew exactly what he needed to say.

As the manuscript came together, it was evident that it could not be a typical sports autobiography. You will find Earl returns to certain key moments and themes, which he uses almost as a kind of passionate chorus, making sure he drives home the point. Earl has plenty to offer about basketball, but this volume is hardly a basketball book. It is a testament. The matters Earl sets out to cover go far beyond sports. He is particularly interested in reaching out to young people of color across the United States—although his larger audience is always all of us.

He refused to do one thing, which will come as no surprise to anyone who knows him: there is little in the way of angry attacks on individuals. Earl—as a black pioneer in a profession that was almost entirely white— had plenty of intensely personal stories involving hurts inflicted by individuals. He would share them with me in a matter-of-fact way, but he always decided against using them. He consciously refrained from using his book as a means of individual payback for old wounds. He was after something larger. In speaking to American truths as he sees them, he is simply asking us to step back and think. He has seen laws and institutions transformed. What he has yet to see are changes in the patterns of deep behavior and belief that form the last great walls of American segregation. To bring them down is a daunting task, but Earl is not one to back away.

After all, this is a guy once called upon to fix the moon.

Acknowledgments

During my life I have acquired many "families" of friends and supporters. I would like to give thanks to:

My Alexandria, Virginia, family, which included my parents and brothers, gave me love, positive values, and support;

My Parker-Gray High School family encouraged my intellectual growth and athletic ability;

My West Virginia State College family embraced me, educated me, and guided me into manhood;

My Central Intercollegiate Athletic Association family taught me sportsmanship and teamwork;

My Washington, D.C., family exposed me to the value of community and perseverance;

My Syracuse, New York, and NBA families assisted me with the transition into a racially diverse America and into the world of professional sports;

My Detroit, Michigan, family provided me with the opportunity to grow and blossom professionally and personally;

My Hall of Fame family recognized me for a professional job well done;

My Fairfield Glade and Crossville, Tennessee, family taught me the fine art of relaxation; and

To my friend Sean Kirst, thank you for your collaboration, vision, and patience.

Finally, a very special note of gratitude and appreciation to my wife, Charlita, and my sons, Kenneth, Kevin, and David, for their love and constant encouragement.

All of you have given me strength and fortitude; I cannot thank you enough.

—Earl Lloyd, September 2009

A word of thanks to many friends. Mike Connor, Charlene Wheeler, and Molly Elliott of the *Syracuse Post-Standard* were generous in their assistance with the location and use of photographs and articles, as were the staff at Earl Lloyd's beloved alma mater, West Virginia State University, especially Sean McAndrews, sports information director, who made a point of coming up with whatever we needed, fast. Onondaga County District Attorney William Fitzpatrick, a disciple of baseball history, allowed us to use a rare photograph of Jackie Robinson in Syracuse.

Le Moyne College in Syracuse provided full access to the materials in its Danny Biasone Collection. The National Basketball Association was helpful in locating photographs, statistics, and archival material, especially in the frantic last days before deadline. Thank you, Zelda.

Many supporting interviews helped with my understanding of Earl's journey. I am particularly grateful to Don "Peewee" Caldwell, Bill Sharman, Dick McGuire, and Bobby Vaughan for their time and insight.

Also, a word of tribute for Eugene "Moon" Williams, jazz aficionado and Earl's dear friend from the Fifteenth Ward in Syracuse. He did not live to see the publication of this book, but he is part of the celebration.

Staff members at the Syracuse University Press were passionate about this project from day one. They handled the manuscript with a gentle touch and endless patience.

Thanks to Mike Streissguth, biographer of Johnny Cash, for his wisdom over coffee in the early stages of this book. Bob McCrone, a neighbor and good friend, gave the manuscript a thorough last-minute read. David Ramsey, a fine writer who is now with the *Colorado Springs Gazette,* shared my reverence for the Nats when we worked in the same building in Syracuse; I miss our regular conversations about Earl, Dolph, and Danny and the team.

Love and thanks, as always, to my wife, Nora, and my children—Sarah, Seamus, and Liam—who remained good-natured about the eternal stack of papers and documents in the dining room. They had my back; without their support, this doesn't happen.

Finally, it is impossible to express my gratitude toward Earl and his wife, Charlita. My long friendship with the Lloyds, in all ways, has been a gift.

—Sean Kirst, September 2009

Moonfixer

Prologue

Lloyd on Obama, Part One

These thoughts were offered by Earl, in the course of many conversations during the presidential campaign of 2008.

I've been watching Obama. I wasn't sure what to think at first. I had to know more. But for this man to survive what he's survived and still be standing tall, that tells me what I need to know. He's one tough guy. First there were the Clintons; she was the odds-on favorite to win the election. And then the folks who opposed Obama . . . they "Rev. Wrighted" him like crazy, and now he's getting more of the same before the general election. None of it gets under his skin. My wife, Charlita, is a genuine worrier. She loves Obama, and she's worried about how this will turn out. In our wildest imaginations, it's still hard to believe this nation might have an African American president. But I keep telling her: For someone to send this guy to this country now, it's got to be part of the divine order. It's a done deal.

Yes, he reminds me a little of Jackie, the way they insult him and try to get him to take the bait. They want him to lose his temper so he seems unfit for the White House. It hasn't happened. That's the most amazing thing, and why so many of us love this man so much. We understand. In some way, at some point, we've all been through the same thing.

No matter what happens in November, it's always going to be about race with a lot of people. If Obama wins, there's going to be a lot of the ruling gentry who feel very nervous. For some, it would be a dramatic change. For others, it would be a traumatic change. But it seems to me you could dig up just about anybody and put them in the White House, and they'd be better than what we've had for the last eight years.

The kids today need to know their history, because once they do they'll understand how Obama epitomizes what it means to be a hero, just by the way he's staying in there, never losing his dignity. There are a lot of people who won't vote for him for scurrilous reasons, and there are too many scurrilous things being said. But I keep reminding myself that this man is one step away from the presidency. In our wildest imaginations, when we were young, we could not imagine a black man in the White House. I'd go to Washington, and I couldn't eat at the restaurants or get a good seat at a ball game! It's almost like this black man was heaven sent. Some people say he's half-black, but in this country there are no half-black people. That's the gospel. If you're a half-black man, you're a black man. It's his message that allows him to go into Iowa and Missouri and Colorado and Kentucky and get people to listen in a way they never listened before.

It's been a long road, and I walked that road along with many, many others, and I can truly appreciate what Barack Obama is going through in this election. It's frustrating, too, a little frightening, to hear some of this anger directed against him, the way people are talking at some of the rallies for Sarah Palin [the Republican candidate for vice president]. I know there are crazy people out there who can't stand the idea of a black man in the White House. The closer we get, the more concerned I become.

We've walked the road for a long time, and the last house on the road is the White House. It is joyful to think about, but a little frightening.

Everywhere I go, I ask the kids if they're registered to vote. Any of them who don't register ought to be ashamed. Some say to me, "My vote won't count." I tell them about Gore—you can't ever forget about Al Gore, and how a handful of votes made all the difference in 2000—but then I tell them that people died so they can have that right to vote. They were hung from trees and burned. They were weighted down with chains and thrown into the river, and you're saying now that using your right to vote doesn't matter? It's all history, and it's why you have to know your history. People paid the ultimate price for that right to vote. When I was a young man, the test they gave you to register was ridiculous. We only got past that with a lot of pain. I tell the kids today, "You don't vote, you don't count. That's all there is."

When they know their history, these kids will really appreciate Barack. His opponents tried to get him angry in the debates. They tried to say he was a pal of terrorists. But they never touched him. He never let them get to him.

If there's a lesson that comes straight from Jackie Robinson, there it is.

We've come a long way, and nothing shows it like this election. But no matter what happens in November, we still have a long way to go. I think maybe the problem is something deep inside each of us, something we can't change until we admit it's there. If you could wave a magic wand and turn all of us green, there'd still be people saying they should be in charge because their feet are larger than everybody else's.

Think about the last couple of years. People like to say things are better with race relations in this nation, and maybe they are, but how about that comedian in the comedy club, the guy who just went off on some black folks in the audience? Later on, he said, "I'm sorry, I didn't mean it," but what he said was coming from somewhere: it's stuff he'd been harboring inside for a long time.

You say these things, and somebody will offer an "if" or a "but." But nobody will ever convince me this is the greatest country in the world until we start dealing with all the "ifs" and "buts."

That should be the lesson of Hurricane Katrina. That pulled the covers off this country. It showed how much we care about poor folks.

Really, not much.

I understand the importance of the middle class, which is what McCain and Obama keep talking about in the election. But I also understand the importance, the imperative, of helping poor people move into the middle class. That takes work, and it's a complicated problem, and we've forgotten about it, almost given up on it. You drive through a city, any city, and you ask, "How can a country as rich as this one have so many homeless people?" It makes no sense. Sean Penn, in *All the King's Men*, he nailed it when he said, "If you don't vote, you don't count."

They voted for Huey Long in Louisiana because no one ever spoke to them in that way before, which is what could happen in this election, too. That's true for whites, not just blacks. For us, what this election means goes beyond explaining.

Ever since the civil rights movement really began, people have been telling us that we should just get over what was done to us, that things are better now, that looking back and being angry won't help anything. I agree that you've got to manage your anger. But I think you're crazy if you forget about looking back, because there are plenty of people in this country who wish things could be that way again. I'm pretty sure you know some of the people I'm talking about.

These are truths that just seem obvious to me. There's something wrong with this picture. I was at a dinner recently with some people who were talking about immigration. They were saying the only way we were going to solve the problem is if we send all the Mexicans back to Mexico. These folks were just giving the Mexicans the blues, all these Mexicans who for years have been doing some of the hardest, most miserable jobs in this country and receiving substandard pay.

You know me. I try to think about what I say before I say it. But I told the people gathered around that table, "Look, I cannot leave this dinner tonight with you folks thinking I approve of what you're saying." The question I asked them is the question I always ask: "When are you going to realize that it's time to vote your interests, instead of your hatreds?"

Now we're in these wars in Iraq and Afghanistan, and they say it's all part of the war on terror. They say we need to use torture and other rough tactics to win, that our only chance is fighting fire with fire. Take it from me: we learned a long time ago that you never win by becoming more like the ones hurting you. Please. Terror? We know all about being terrorized: Lynchings. Beatings. Burnings. Getting thrown into jail without fair trials. Terror was the whole fear. Terror is what kept us from doing the things any normal human being would want to do. Billie Holiday, a singer, saw the remains of a hanging. That's what caused her to sing the song "Strange Fruit." White people didn't know what it was about, but we knew. That was always with us, at every minute of the day.

Think about Emmett Till, a kid who was tortured and murdered by people who went to church, who called themselves Christians. Terror is terror, and always has the same result. And once you walk down that torture road, it's hard to walk back. We know better than anyone just how far we've come in this country, but we also know some of the hardest truths.

This is how much I think of Barack Obama: if he becomes president, I think he can do more than anyone's done to overcome all of that. But I think he'll win for one reason that has nothing to do with color: in these times, people will finally vote their interests. There are a lot of people who are going to look at what's happened in the last eight years and vote what's best for them, even if they have to use their other hand to push their fingers to his lever.

It's hard not to get your hopes too high, but I have to step back and remember how unbelievable it seems that Barack Obama has made it this far. There was a time when no one, in their wildest dreams, could have imagined a black man in the White House. You've got to really think about that; when I was a kid, I couldn't swim in the public pool. They made me swim in the river. The idea of growing up to serve in the White House? Never. It wasn't part of the equation. It was hard enough for one of us just to go and vote.

There's a long road from Joe Louis and Jackie to Barack Obama, and a lot of people walked it who lived and died without getting their fair

3. The home of Earl and Charlita Lloyd is filled with mementos and works of art linked to the Obama presidency. On the night of the inauguration, they hosted a joyous party at which guests could have their photos taken next to a life-size image of the new president. (Photo by Joe Crowell Jr., courtesy of Earl and Charlita Lloyd)

chance, folks you'll never hear about today. I know I've been called a pioneer, but there were a lot of people ready to be pioneers who got stopped along the way. If Barack Obama wins, this is the only claim I make:

Like a lot of others, I spent some time on that same road.

1

Jackie

Over the past twenty years, as Earl Lloyd finally began to be recognized nationally for the magnitude of his accomplishments, he often heard a familiar comparison from journalists, historians, and everyday fans. It is a comparison he refuses to accept, for reasons that say everything about Earl.

I get asked about it everywhere I go. Almost sixty years ago, I walked out onto the basketball court in Rochester for a game I don't even remember all that well. There are plenty of games that in memory seem much more important, but that is the game that put me down in history: the first black American to play in the National Basketball Association.

All these years later, I think about it, and I want to start this book with one thought. I've always said, "Don't compare me to Jackie Robinson." I'll always take polite umbrage when people bring that up. It's an honor, but I don't deserve that comparison. Jackie was unique. What he went through, no one should have to go through.

Someone asked me once: What was the most important achievement for you in basketball? And I said, "Getting there." Because by the time I reached the NBA, I'd already overcome most of the hurdles, even if I didn't realize it. The game was ready at that moment, at that point, for some real change. I didn't really see myself at that point in time as representing what was about to come, but you look at who's playing professional basketball now, and you look at professional basketball then, and sure, you've got to stop and think. For me, in 1950, the most important thing was just getting to that first camp with all these guys of renown, and then sticking around.

I'm at a point now where people will look back on those days, on what I did, and they'll say: "You're the Jackie Robinson of basketball."

Part of that, I think, is because I'm still here. If Sweetwater Clifton or Chuck Cooper were here with me, maybe it would feel a little different, a little better, if the three of us could sit together and reflect. Because all three of us went into the NBA in 1950. But I think they would agree with me on this: I can't accept it when anyone compares me to Jackie. He was my idol, and I was in an all-black college when he broke in, and you can't imagine what he meant to us—although I'd have to put Joe Louis in there with him, too.

You think about those times, and what we couldn't do: In college, at West Virginia State, we'd go on long road trips and couldn't stop to use a restroom. In college, a lot of times, we'd sleep on cots in the gyms of the schools we were playing. One time we were getting on a bus to go to North Carolina, and the bus driver told us to get to the back. Our college coach, Mark Cardwell, stood up to the driver. He told us to stay in front, and we saw that driver reaching for his belt, and we wanted to say, "Coach. It's all right. We'll sit on the bumper." Because in the end we all knew it was a fight we couldn't win.

Joe Louis—he did all our fighting for us when we couldn't. Joe came through at a time when you didn't dare hit a white person, no matter how bad things got, no matter what was said to you. You've got to think about that, and really appreciate what I'm saying: people could address us as less than human, could speak about us like animals, and there was nothing we could do about it. And then—in that environment—here's Joe getting paid to knock white people out. He's getting paid to hit white guys in the face. When he hit someone, man, I thought my knuckles were right inside that glove. He was the only guy in my time who could legitimately beat up a white person, and he did it all the time.

The folks who ran the fights, they were constantly looking for a white hope, and time after time, Joe would dash that hope.

When Joe Louis fought, everything stopped in black neighborhoods. When he won, people ran outside, they celebrated, they banged pots and pans, and you can understand why. That was a crazy time. In so many other ways, we had absolutely no recourse. Those folks who kept us down, the folks we could never strike back against, Joe was getting paid to knock them out.

I was no Joe Louis. I was no Jackie Robinson. I appreciate everyone who says that, but I remember those times. Now Jackie, when I think of him, all I can think about is everything that he went through. It's important to remember where baseball stood at that time. There were great black athletes playing basketball on teams like the Globetrotters or the New York Rens, and there were great black athletes playing college football and basketball. But baseball was the game everyone played in this nation, and the whole country followed Major League Baseball, and even as young black kids we knew all about the Negro League stars.

The Major Leagues were all white. If I went in to watch a Negro League game at Griffith Stadium in Washington, D.C., I could sit anywhere I wanted. If I went to see a Senators game in the American League, they put me out in the bleachers. I couldn't sit with the ruling gentry. That was in the nation's capital, watching the national pastime. You want a clear example of how it was in the country, all you have to do is think about what it was like to go to a baseball game not so far from the White House.

That's how it was. Everyone knew it, and everyone followed baseball, so if you made a change in baseball, you could change the country. So Jackie faced bigger problems than I ever faced when he was trying to break in. Basketball had fewer problems because many of the white guys in basketball had experience playing against blacks. And most basketball players in the early NBA were college graduates, which made a difference. In baseball, most players—especially from the southern environs—did not. The adjustment in basketball was a lot easier for guys like us than it was for a guy like Jackie Robinson.

Jackie played in a league where almost no one went to college, and a lot of these guys in the majors came from rural communities in the Deep South. I played in a game where the ball knows no prejudice; everybody touches it, and everybody touches each other. If you say something to me, if you try something on me, sooner or later you've got to deal with me, in a way the referee can't always see. I could throw a pick in a special way that might make you think again about the words you used.

Jackie was alone. They could throw the ball at his head, and he couldn't do anything about it. He wasn't a pitcher. What recourse did he have? They could say anything they wanted, do pretty much anything they wanted, and he had to stand there and take it. Baseball wasn't basketball. You're out there by yourself. Dixie Walker led the league in hitting for Brooklyn, and when he found out about Jackie, he said, "I ain't playing with no niggers." And Branch Rickey, the guy who signed Jackie, said, "Dixie, you're right. You're going to Pittsburgh."

Jackie handled name-calling and death threats like you can't believe, and he couldn't hit back. The story goes that Rickey took him into a room and said every foul and terrible thing you can say to a man about him or his family, and then said to Jackie, "Can you take that on the field without striking back?" Here's a guy with as much fire in his belly as anyone who ever played the game, and they're telling him to eat it, not to retaliate. He had some of his own teammates vilifying him. The only refuge he had was he went home at night to his wife, Rachel. I wish I had met him, just to thank him, and I still hope to meet Rachel someday. Our paths never crossed, but for him to survive in that arena, it was just amazing, and he made it that much easier for the rest of us. Those are handprints, big handprints. I carry them today.

Here's the tragedy, and you can spread it out over hundreds of years of our history: all these people with talents and gifts they could have shared with everyone, people whose gifts were buried under sheer stupidity. I always worry that all this talk about who came first makes it easier to forget about them, because I was just lucky. The door opened for me; it was ready to open. But I came through it with handprints all over me, the handprints of folks who never got the chance, just like Barack Obama has handprints all over him.

Before Jackie, we used to go to Griffith Stadium to watch the Senators of the American League and the Homestead Grays, a great team from the Negro Leagues. Like I said, with the Senators, they made us sit in the sun, or way down the foul lines. We were segregated, and we sat in the segregated section. For the Grays, we could sit anyplace we'd like, which meant we could watch guys like Josh Gibson up close. The gentry never got to see Josh or Satchel Paige or Cool Papa Bell or any of those great players in their prime, and they were all great players. The gentry thought they were cheating us, but I think people who didn't get to see them play were cheated even worse.

4. Addressing the crowd about a favorite theme—the "handprints" of those who have touched his life for the better—during Earl's Hall of Fame enshrinement in 2003. (Courtesy of Earl and Charlita Lloyd)

People say nice things to me all the time, but nothing I did can compare to what Jackie had to endure. In his prime, he might not even have been the best player in the Negro Leagues, even if he was one of the greatest athletes in the world: A great football player, a world-class track and field man. He started on the basketball team at UCLA. There were other great players, men like Josh Gibson, great players who never got the attention they deserved. Josh, if you ever saw him, you knew he could hit it a long way. But Jackie was the best fit for the situation he would have to endure.

Funny thing is, baseball was my favorite game. I pitched for Parker-Gray High School and again in college at West Virginia State. The Brooklyn Dodgers scouted me in the summer of 1950, when Branch Rickey was still running the team. They invited me to a tryout camp at Cambridge, Maryland. I was six-foot-five, 220, with a rubber arm, and I could throw it hard. But I was wild. The only problem was that it was going to take some work to keep me from killing people. Not long after I went to that camp, I went into the service, and baseball went out of my mind.

But a couple of years later, when I was getting out of the army, I got a letter from Rex Bowen, a scout who was with Pittsburgh. Rickey had gone to the Pirates and taken Bowen with him. They were interested in me launching a baseball career in Enid, Oklahoma. Enid was a "sundown town": if you were black, you'd better be inside, doors locked, by sundown. I found that very unattractive. And I knew it might take a long time, if ever, to make the majors as a pitcher, and I had already tested the basketball thing, and I knew I had a chance to succeed. I spurned Pittsburgh's offer.

I went with basketball. Would I have believed, almost sixty years later, that black kids would pretty much forget about baseball and put all their dreams into basketball? When I was a kid, you couldn't have dreamed it.

But there were a lot of things I couldn't dream.

2

Lemonade!

For years, I've had a lot of people telling me I need to do a book. My friends and family tell me I need to do it, because of what I've done and the things I've seen. That's been cause for a lot of thought, and I want to start this with something that might shock you, something I'll come back to as we go through this thing.

Segregation served me well. And I think there is something there, a kind of secret, that people need to understand.

I grew up in Alexandria, Virginia, a cradle of segregation, right across the river from our nation's capital. During my time, during all my school years, the most respected people in the neighborhood were the teachers. None of us got in trouble. You couldn't afford to get in trouble. The folks we respected the most were the teachers. We saw them every day, and they saw our parents around the neighborhood, and we knew they'd be telling our parents what we were doing. But we didn't just listen to them out of fear. We listened to them because we wanted to please them, because we knew they wanted the best for us. For years, we were handed lemons.

Because of teachers who truly cared, it became lemonade.

Do you understand? This is why segregation served us well. Our teachers were all black, and there was a benefit to that. Now, I'm not saying white teachers can't teach black kids, but this was a love affair. These were all-black schools, and these teachers knew any chance we had out in the world was incumbent on what they gave us in the classroom. And they were receptive to that challenge.

They lived the same things we lived. They had been stopped by the same things stopping us. Every teacher who taught me was serious. They wanted one thing, and that was for us to find a way out, and there was only one way to do it: knowledge. Basketball was my path, but basketball would not have been there for me if not for my teachers.

To me, today, one of the biggest problems we have in our schools is that teachers don't get that kind of reverence and respect. Our parents taught us that anyone in authority deserved respect—and by authority, I mean adult black authority, because you did everything you could to stay away from white authority.

Our teachers knew exactly what would give us a chance. They provided it every day, and they knew our parents wanted us to have it, too. I'm old school, a believer that we're all products of our environment. The people who sit across from you at the dinner table on a daily basis, especially when you're a child, have a tremendous effect on you for the rest of your life. That's why I know how hard it is for some people to change the way they think. So many folks grow up hearing things—hateful things—from their parents at that table, and then they take all that out into the world. Be honest. If you love your mother and father, it is a hard thing to give up the things your parents felt and believed.

So there are times, even now, when I will be sitting with someone and they will be saying one thing about the way they see the world, and I can feel something else is going on deep inside them. They'll say that's not the way they are, that they don't carry any bias against anyone, but they'll look hard for any example that will justify the way they really feel. I know what their parents taught them is still living in there, and that is still the hardest thing for any human being to change.

Not that any of it is an excuse for putting someone else on the wrong end of that anger. Looking back on it, you've got to wonder: how could they hate Dr. Martin Luther King Jr.? Wasn't he saying all the right things about what it meant to be Christian? Didn't he live out the idea of peace? All he talked about was loving your enemies and praying for your enemies. Isn't that what Christianity means? How much do you have to hear at that kitchen table to hate someone like him?

The night he was murdered, I was at Bethune-Cookman, a historically black college in Daytona Beach, Florida. I was giving a speech. It was so tragic, so shocking . . . but in a way, I always knew something like that could happen. You'd understand why I could feel that way, if you grew up where I grew up.

We knew when we were children that what our teachers had to offer was exactly what we needed, and our parents knew it, too. They did their best to enforce it. Disrupt a class, and you knew your parents were going to find out, and you knew you'd get killed once you got home. I did some crazy things, and my parents told me, "You want to be a buffoon, put on a dunce's cap and face the wall. But it is totally unacceptable for you to deprive the other kids who want to learn."

I remember I had a hell of a doctor, and his name was Charles West, an old football player who'd gone to a little school in Pennsylvania. I think he was maybe the first black athlete to go to his university, and we bonded. When we went to see him, he'd spend a little more time with me and he'd show some interest in me, and that means more than you know. When you are in a hard place, and you're around people who are genuinely concerned about you, that's a very good thing, maybe the most important thing, and I wonder how many kids have a Dr. West today.

What our kids are going through now is a monumental problem, but it comes from a simple place. Whether you want to admit it or not, a lot of the same attitudes that I saw when I was growing up are still out there, blocking the road, those same beliefs people first heard across their dinner tables. It's harder now, because people are better at hiding them or express them in different ways. But how can we really move forward until those attitudes get set aside?

If you gave me a magic wand, and said, "You've got one shot at fixing all of this," I'd say, "We've got to start caring about each other." As a people we made a wrong turn somewhere, and we can't get back, and it all comes back to caring for one another. Because basketball wasn't really why I made it out. That was only the path I followed. I made it because so many people cared about me. If there's one point to take out of this book, that's it.

At the Hall of Fame in Springfield, Massachusetts, when I gave my acceptance speech, I talked about my life as being an incredible journey. Think about that. It wasn't that I was an incredible person, but only that

I came up during incredible times. Incredible times make for incredible people, like the ones who surrounded me, and they always made sure I got what I needed.

Our parents couldn't ride in the front of the bus. They couldn't get good jobs. They couldn't swim in public pools. They had to swim in the river. They even had to use a "black" water fountain. That was their life, and it wasn't going to change. All they had to root for was us. We didn't have a decent school building, or a decent gymnasium. We had nothing. My family started out in a house that didn't have indoor plumbing, and later on we moved into a project that did, a place where I had my own room. Today, you say "project," and people say "ghetto." But to us, that could have been the Taj Mahal. That was it.

If someone came to our house, at any time, the place was clean enough that you could have eaten off the floor. My parents couldn't give us much. They made sure they gave us that. And at game time, if I looked in the stands, my parents would be there.

This is why I'm always talking about handprints. Take a look at yourself at the end of any journey, and you've got the handprints of others all over you. You're fooling yourself if you think you do it by yourself. My parents were always telling me, "No one's better than you." That's the message I got over my dinner table. Every day, it was reinforced. You bought into it, and you tried to remember it years later when you walked into a locker room filled with white guys, some of the most famous basketball players in America, when you hadn't even had a real conversation with a white man in your life.

You could not quit. You could not give up. You had to remember all the people who gave so much to get you there.

You see what I'm saying—why segregation served us well? I wouldn't wish it on anyone, and I thank God it's gone, but it made us look out for one another, and it kept us together as a community.

I've got three sons—Kenneth, Kevin, and David—and four grandchildren. A lot of trials and tribulations went into all the stories in this book. But my grandchildren need to know. They have to understand that in their lives, in any life, there's going to be adversity, and you're going to have to develop real character, or you won't be able to overcome your troubles.

5. Earl with his sons *(left to right)*, Kevin, Kenneth, and David, at his Naismith Memorial Basketball Hall of Fame induction in 2003. (Photo by Carolyn Briscoe, courtesy of Earl and Charlita Lloyd)

All the skills in the world, all the wonderful gifts and characteristics, they mean absolutely nothing if you're not courageous. Courage doesn't mean being unafraid. Courage means being afraid, and going ahead anyway. The kids are all caught up in these ideas of "manhood," but they've got it confused. I look at the kids now and I think, "Just getting up and going to school and trying—that's courage, that's character." Because I think if people stop and really think, these kids are afraid.

So were we. But we knew who we'd be letting down if we didn't keep going.

I look at what's happening with these kids in the cities, and it just breaks my heart. It is amazing to me, with all this new technology, all these new ways of communicating, how this violence and suffering only get worse. There's something wrong today with the way people raise their children and want to be their friends. We can't be friends with our kids, because when you've got to tell people, any people, to do what they don't want to do, they can't be your friends. If they're your friends, they won't do it.

As kids, we did what we were told. My high school coach, Coach Louis Johnson, was the nicest guy in the world. He would say, "I'm not always right, but I'm always in charge, and if you're going to play for me, you're going to accept it." When the man said we were leaving at eight, we were leaving at eight, no questions asked. The folks who weren't there got left behind, and the message was bigger than any sport or any game. I played three sports for the man, and by his account I played them fairly well. But he demanded something of us: you can't be a star athlete in your high school and be a damn fool. It doesn't mix. We just weren't allowed to be that way. One of Coach Johnson's main teachings—and we heard it everywhere—was that you're only special if other folks think you're special. That's where today's kids need that courage. Because somehow you've got to find your way to the folks who can lift you up.

For me, it started with my parents. Each morning they went to jobs that wore them down, and at the end of the day they were always tired. Their consolation, their joy, was what we were doing. We knew that. We gave them something to cheer about. My dad was a quiet, hardworking guy. He and my mother always told us that they'd be judged by the way we conducted ourselves. My mother's last statement every day when I walked out the door was, "Do not embarrass this family." She wasn't talking about winning or losing. She was talking about conduct.

That kind of teaching shaped me, from birth into high school into college. The hands that molded me were the hands of people who really cared about me. Today, for a lot of kids, that isn't the case. Too many people don't care about who they embarrass, and that's the way they raise their children—or maybe they don't raise them—and that's the way you see those children playing the game. In my day, if you saw a situation where you knew your parents wouldn't want you to be there, you got out of it.

If you can't find a role model under your own roof, you've got a big problem. So you take kids coming out of that situation, if they run into a coach who's only interested in winning, then that problem becomes even bigger. We're seeing that much too often.

People ask me, in my career, who influenced me the most. Talk to me for ten minutes, and you'll know: my mother. She made life easier, even then. You knew she loved us to death. You knew she wouldn't tell us to do anything detrimental. This is where segregation served us, in a way I

6. Earl, with his trophy and ring, at the Hall of Fame enshrinement in 2003. (Courtesy of Earl and Charlita Lloyd)

just wish these kids could see. We could not survive if we factionalized. We hung tough. You knew where to go, where not to go, when not to go. The racial stuff was so crazy it was stupid. But it was real, and it could get you killed.

If you saw the movie *Remember the Titans*, it was made in Alexandria, my hometown. That took place in, what, 1971? The major difference between us and the kids of that era was that at least they got a chance to prove themselves on the field. We never played against the kids from the white schools. Like I say, I did not have a real conversation with a white person until I was an adult. The evil of it was that no matter how much the people who love you reassure you, you're always questioning your worth as a person. You'd go to the back of the bus. You'd see the sign saying, "Colored only." That seeps in. I think, for many kids, it's still seeping in today. It's why a lot of them never make it. They see the messages all around them, even if no one paints it on a sign.

So when a young black kid from Virginia ends up in an NBA camp, you don't ask the question out loud, but you wonder, "Do I really belong here?"

That changed once they threw up the ball.

3

Bootstraps, Anyone?

I grew up in the cradle of segregation: Alexandria, Virginia. It's part of a beautiful state, if they decide to let you use it. I just don't have a lot of fond memories of Virginia, because of the way I was made to feel, but let me try to separate this out: I have nothing but fond memories of childhood, because of the people who surrounded me.

Let's not lie to ourselves. Virginia is a place where—not so long ago— the ruling gentry didn't want to desegregate their schools. They threatened to shut them down rather than having black kids sitting next to their kids. But I'm still around, and a lot of the folks who felt that way about me are still around, and now a lot of them smile and shake my hand and talk about the Hall of Fame.

But if they had the chance to make everything go back to the way it was—if someone handed them that magic wand and told them they really had the chance to roll it back—would they do it? You tell me. What do you think?

Reflections like that can bring up anger, but we were taught to handle our anger when we were young. Some could, some couldn't. If you couldn't, you were through. Even on the court, I had to handle the anger. You see parents and teammates and teachers get treated throughout your life like second-class citizens, and yes, it has some effect. The anger's there. You're on a corner—one of the few places in town they let you go—and the cops come and say, "Clear the corner," and you know they're only clearing it for one reason.

Yes, you feel the anger.

For me, growing up, it didn't start crystallizing until about the tenth grade. At that age there's a transformation going on, and you suddenly realize how all these folks are perpetuating a hoax by saying you're "separate but equal."

I used to stand and look at George Washington High School—or as close as I could get, because they didn't want you there—and then I'd think of how we had zero facilities at my high school, Parker-Gray: no gym, no baseball field, no stadium. We played our basketball in this tiny auditorium, and we used to joke around that we got our school colors wrong. Ours were blue and white; we should have adopted the colors from George Washington so maybe we could get their old equipment when they threw it out, if the administrators there would have even given it to us.

Despite all that, I'm telling you, I was lucky. Education was important to my family, and anytime I didn't try in school I knew I'd have a problem at home. My mother knew what we all ought to understand now: if you can't read, you've got a serious problem. This is the information age, but what good is information—how do you digest it—if you can't read it? Look, I've got a warm spot for teachers, period. Our teachers, I'll tell you this, they were all from our community, and they knew they were our only chance for getting out, and they cared about us, almost like we were their own kids. Teachers today—I know a lot of them care. But can it really be the same when they're living twenty-five miles away, in a different world, from the neighborhoods where they teach?

The other problem, the one that really puts teachers up against it: if it's not important to a kid's parent, it's not going to be important to a kid. And too many parents don't really care about education. How they can forget, how they can't understand, I don't know. That's where we failed, where we made that wrong turn. No parent should ever forget the way it was.

I never knew my paternal grandparents. My dad, Theodore Lloyd, was a very quiet guy; some might call him nondescript. He never talked much about his childhood. He was Alexandria born and bred, but he was a guy you could really respect because he got up early in the morning and went to the coal yard, and by the time he got back and cleaned up and ate it was just about time to go to bed. Day after day, he did that for us. You know, he had the dirtiest job, shoveling loads of coal on and off of trucks, and he didn't even want me to come visit him down there. Think of that job. You're cracking all day, those trucks are coming and going, and he did that for us. You think it wasn't his dream for us to have something else? He didn't get to see all of my games, because we played in the afternoon and he was working, and if he took off he'd lose his job. But I know he was always glad I did well.

I think that might have been the hardest part, seeing what segregation did to someone like him. All these folks today, you hear them talking about how folks should pull themselves up by the bootstraps, and you know who they're talking about. They're talking about us. But what about if the gentry won't let you wear those boots? When someone says, "I know how you feel," I always think: You can't. You can't until someone tells you that you can't do this or can't do that, or you've got to go to the back of this bus, and if you don't do it something very bad is going to happen. If you don't live that, you just can't understand. That's how my father lived, every day of his life. Segregation was degradation, but he got up and went to work.

My mother—she would always come to my games. She was a farm girl from a little town called Hamilton, Virginia. Her people were working farmers, and I guess the city was always a little fast for her. My mother used to send me and my brothers to stay on the farm with her family for two weeks, and I'd pray, "Lord, help me, please somebody, get me out of here," because there wasn't anything to do except work on that farm. We ate good and we got plenty of rest, but it was not a place we wanted to stay. Alexandria was not a teeming metropolis, but it was big enough compared to where my mother came from; Alexandria was close to D.C., and at least there were some things that we could do. We played softball in the morning and football in the afternoon, and the funny thing, looking back on it, was that basketball was third.

Our parents and our teaching staff, they looked at the way things were, and they were dedicated to one proposition: you're going to get an education, and no one can ever take that away from you. One difference for us, I think, from the way it is for a lot of the kids today is that we had stable homes. Whoever said your parents are your first and best teachers had it right: they gave us all the things we needed at that time. We always were in good shape for food and clothes, and they always seemed to have enough to feed my friends. My parents had a tremendous affinity for young people. All they wanted—for me, for my two older brothers, for my friends—was for us to have a chance. They weren't middle class, but they had middle-class values, and that's how they steered us. It was impressed on us that just because someone is treating you in a way you shouldn't be treated—and we knew that was going to happen a lot—you couldn't fold your tent.

We were well schooled in survival tactics, in making sure we didn't get ourselves into situations where we could get hurt, or worse. If we were on a corner, and a cop came by, we were gone. You didn't wait for something to be said. We knew how to avoid getting hurt, because our parents and teachers learned the hard way how to avoid getting hurt.

My mother, she had me ready for college. Kids today, a lot of them don't eat decently, and that matters. It can make you or break you. You go to school hungry, or you go to school full of nothing but sugar, and how are you going to work? My house, let me tell you, always smelled good. My mother could really burn. Man, she could cook. My dad was an easygoing, quiet guy, but my mother was the disciplinarian, the point person for family business.

She allowed the house to be the kind of place that was a hangout for my friends. She had a tremendous affinity for kids who were struggling, and that can mean everything. If you don't get that love at home, you've got to get it someplace, because a kid will do a lot for someone if he knows he's loved. Any friend of mine was always welcome. My mother taught us: you're judged by how you treat your guests. In my town, if you treated your guests badly, it got around. People knew.

My mother was also very practical. The night before a game, eight thirty, nine o'clock, she'd be asking, "Don't you have a game tomorrow?" The response was, "Yes, ma'am," and then you headed for bed. Because she'd say to me, "Word gets back to me you're a pretty good player, and if you don't play up to your potential, your team will definitely have to do a lot more to win." She felt responsibility not just for me but for the team. At sixteen, seventeen years old, on the nights before a game, she'd say the word, and I'd go to bed.

My parents were big on that message: if you're a high school athlete, and you're going someplace where the people don't know you, the only way they'll know your family is through you. I'll always remember one of her most famous quotes. I was someplace where I shouldn't have been, and I said, "Yes, I was there, but I wasn't doing anything." And she said, "If you aren't in the picture, you can't get framed."

She knew. In Alexandria, you didn't even want to be standing around a crime scene when the police showed up. If they needed the criminal who did it, they'd find him. Understand? My parents taught me those things; they were the rules to live by for any child, the rules of self-protection. In that way, I really did have a great childhood. Great parents, great teachers, great times with my friends on the playground. That's why our sports teams at Parker-Gray were so good. The more we played, the more adept we became. All we had was basketball, softball, and the playground. We couldn't go anyplace else. There were no jobs for us, not even any swimming pools for us; if you were white, you got the pool. We got the river. The Potomac, at that time, you don't know how terrible it was, full of human waste and everything else. But if you're a kid, and it's hot, you want to go swimming. Almost every year we'd lose a kid in there until finally, after three or four kids drowned, they came up with a makeshift pool.

Anger? Of course. But what got us out was love.

That's it. That's how segregation served me well. The only way. I'll say it again, and I say it all the time, and I know you think it's crazy. But the challenges I faced as a child, and the people who helped me find a way through them, made everything after that seem almost easy.

In Alexandria, it was as clear as day and night. You wouldn't believe it today. We'd be walking to school, and their nice school buses would drive by, taking their kids to this beautiful building with a nice gym. They had the new books, the new uniforms, all the new equipment. We didn't even have athletic fields.

I can't recall the moment I understood as a child, but one day you realized. And from then on, you knew. You saw the signs saying "Whites only" and "Colored only," and if you were on the wrong end of that, you knew. That was a cavern you could fall into very easily, a place that could eat you alive if you weren't being constantly reassured about the kind of person that you were. As you got older, as a lot of things crystallized, you were like an automaton about a lot of it: you were going to go to the back of the bus, or the front of the train, or you were going to use the woods when you were traveling by car because you couldn't use their restrooms.

You just knew. It was programmed deep inside you. You pick up the newspaper, and your team is winning games and winning championships, but your school isn't in there, not even being mentioned, and you know: It's the ruling gentry. You're on the wrong end of it. You learn that, and if you're surrounded by the wrong people, if you don't have the support, that's enough to finish you long before you get started. Because this perceived lack of value gets reinforced even by the people you care about the most, and I think you can argue that's been handed down; a lot of it is still going on today. You figure you don't have a reason to learn anything else, which is how I think many of these kids feel right now. They think: What does it matter? The people you care about are telling you and showing you they have no hope. And if you believe you're not going anyplace, then learning only makes it that much harder, because then you learn what you can't have. The difference now is that kids are taught to feel that way unofficially. When I was a kid, it was the law of the land. The people in charge wanted us to believe we were inferior, that there was no way out, that we might as well give up. If you didn't give up, you could get yourself in big trouble, fast. I look back now, and those were crazy times. Insane.

The difference for me, and for many of my friends, was being surrounded by people who gave us hope, people who refused to surrender to despair, people who put all their faith in us. In that way, a way the ruling gentry could never understand and certainly never intended, segregation was a gift. They couldn't take away my mind, and they couldn't take away the way I was loved. Don't get me wrong: I saw a lot of people give up. A lot of people I cared about were lost along the way, and I understand what happened to them. You learn you have no chance of making it in the larger society, and one day it just overwhelms you, especially when you watch all these people on the other side, the people who are doing it to you, the people holding you down, and they're going to church on Sunday. You just stop and ask, "How can a person go to church and then treat another person in that way?"

Years later, after I was inducted into the basketball Hall of Fame, someone came up to me and said, "Your speech was amazing." I told them, the speech wasn't amazing. The story is amazing. If you were a black kid born in Virginia in 1928, at that moment in history, the chances of you doing anything unusual with your life were just about zero. Everything was set up to keep you down. They didn't even want you thinking about it. And I went from that to the pinnacles of my sport—an NBA championship, being a head coach, and then the Hall of Fame. You know why? Because, from the minute I was born, a lot of folks cared about me. Even now, you ask me my worst nightmare in life—and I'm in my eighties now!—and that nightmare would be letting down these people who put so much faith in me.

These guys coming up now, so many times, whether they make it or they don't, they say, "I don't need anybody." They don't understand. Nothing happens for them without someone else. They wouldn't even be in a position to say that without someone else. And if they choose to try to get by without someone else, then they choose to go back to the same place, and the same fate, that everyone in our community was looking at in 1928. That's crazy. They're turning their backs on the people who came before, the ones who gave their lives to give these kids a chance.

When you start, you've got to start with the birthplace, and that was Alexandria, Virginia, April 3, 1928. I held on for a few days, maybe because I didn't want to be born on April 1. I had two older brothers; I was the baby. They had a birth certificate for me at the Alexandria hospital. But I don't know if they allowed black folks to be born in there. If I had to guess, I would guess I was born in the house.

We were not people of means. Electricity? No. Not at first. A lot of folks had plumbing; a lot of us didn't have plumbing. In my house, there was no indoor plumbing. What we had was an outside facility that flushed.

Alexandria, black and white, was a city of enclaves. I lived in a part of town referred to as "the Berg," and when I was a kid the Berg was a tough part of town, meaning that it was a part of town where most of the kids who lived there did not finish high school. There was a fertilizer plant and some coal yards, some of the harshest, toughest jobs you could find. For the parents in my neighborhood, the fertilizer plant and coal yards were not an option for their kids. Whoever coined the phrase "A mind is a terrible thing to waste" was thinking of places like the Berg.

The only kids who got out and went to the black colleges were kids with high talent, scholarship-level talent, or the kids whose parents were professionals. I had a lot of classmates, particularly girls, who were just very, very bright, and it was criminal that they didn't get a chance to go on. A whole lot of good minds fell by the wayside. A lot of people who would have flourished in a college setting never got that chance.

Some years back, my hometown had a day for me, a monumental thing for Alexandria. Given the kind of life we had there, I had misgivings about going back. The high school now is named for T. C. Williams—you remember it, maybe, from *Remember the Titans*—and T. C. Williams was the superintendent of schools when I was there. He was not a standup person for us. He ruled over a system that treated us as if we were not alive. We had nothing—not a gym, not a baseball stadium, nothing. What we had, what saved us, was a magical coach named Louis Johnson.

T. C. Williams, for us, was a figment of our imagination. We never saw him in our schools. Books, uniforms, anything we needed, we always came up short. Maybe that's why we were so good in sports. We were driven by what was taken away from us. Anyway, I got invited back, and the festivities were going to be held at T. C. Williams High School. I was ready to tell them, "No, thank you, but I will not be honored in a building that carries that man's name." But in any household you need a saner voice, and my wife is our saner voice. Charlita said, "If your feelings are that strong, don't go," but she also said, "You know, you'll disappoint a lot of people who watched you grow up, people who played with you and supported you. And you're sure you're not going to go?" Now, there are times when a woman like Charlita sounds as if she is giving you a choice, when in reality she is saying what she knows you should do, and you know you'd better appreciate the wisdom.

I went. We walked into the gym before the game began, and on the right-hand side is the new Alexandria, the grandkids and great-grandchildren of the folks I never knew. On the other side are guys I played ball with, my people, their children and grandchildren, and then there are people who remember me and they're with their children and grandchildren, and both

7. Earl and Charlita on their wedding day, 1978. (Courtesy of Earl and Charlita Lloyd)

sides of that gym give me a tremendous standing ovation. In Alexandria, this place where I once couldn't walk on many streets. If that doesn't grab me by the Adam's apple, what else would?

Thomas Wolfe said, "You can't go home again," but I beg to differ. This homecoming was sweet. There were six guys there I played ball with. Some of them I'd known since we were in kindergarten, and they understood. We've got that history. This is what I'm saying: I went into the Hall of Fame, but I felt every one of them with me when I did. They were the same as me, saw the same things, lived the same things, and they were just tremendous athletes. And when they threw this day for me, these guys were standing there applauding. Now, that's tall cotton. It's a proud moment. These were my people, folks who I admired, and they're bestowing this honor on me? Naming the court after me? They can say that, but they really named it after all of us, because you cannot come from whence I came, and get to where I am today, without a whole lot of hands being all over you. You accept the honor, but you accept it on behalf of a whole lot of people who went through the same things.

The next day a young lady from a television station interviewed me. She said, "You don't talk about yourself much," and she asked me what accomplishment I cherish most. I told her, "Awards are beautiful, but at the end of every day it's how people view you as a person that really counts." And I was thinking of all these folks who knew me before college, before the NBA, before anything, really. They had a little ceremony at halftime, with all these people who'd known me over the years. What that group was saying to me, what I hope they were saying, is that maybe I became the kind of person they expected me to be. If so, that's it. That's my accomplishment, bigger than the Hall of Fame, bigger than anything. Because that's what drove us from the minute we could really understand. Bring that back as a goal today, on the part of the community, on the part of the parents, on the part of the kids, and the problems would be solved. No one would be shooting each other. Because those expectations make sure you can never rest or take life for granted, not until the day you die.

My folks, as I said, were not educated people. My dad worked in a coal yard. He loaded trucks and unloaded trucks, day after day. This wasn't skilled labor. This was work, backbreaking work. My mother was a domestic. She cleaned white people's houses. During the war, I remember there was a torpedo plant for submarines, and during that stretch my mother worked at that plant. Those were the role models I grew up with: in the morning, you get up and you go to work, and what gets you through it is thinking about coming home to your family. Again, I ask you, given the chances I was given, how was I going to let my parents down? When I had the chance to go to college because I was skilled at a game, when I got a chance to make a living playing that game, how was I not going to give my all to it? To do anything else would have been an insult to my parents, to the sweat and tears they shed just to give me that chance.

Anybody who's a friend of your parents, they become members of your extended family. So I had people across Alexandria who took special pains to reassure me of my worth as a person, even when I was living with all this "colored this" and "colored that" and you didn't walk here and you couldn't walk there. The reality of it doesn't hit you for a while. When you're a little kid, you listen to your parents, and you learn where to go and where not to go and how to interact, and it's what you do because it's what you're told to. That goes on up until ninth or tenth grade, when you realize how you're really at the mercy of the ruling gentry. Did anyone really believe Parker-Gray was equal with the other high schools? We all knew. To say otherwise was a joke.

Once it hit me, it ate at me. I could not understand. These kids, my friends, were the nicest people in the world. I asked a preacher once, "Maybe you can help me: what have we done as a people to deserve this treatment?" I said this has been going on for hundreds of years, and I wanted to know how long we'd have to endure it. His answer was that everything is part of God's test. So let me ask, after two hundred years, can someone tell me if we've passed?

Looking back, grade school was gravy. You had no fears. You might live four blocks from some whites, but that was four long blocks, you know? When I was a child, a real famous person lived four blocks away. I used to see John L. Lewis walking his dog. This guy was the president of the United Mine Workers, a union man, champion of the working man, but I wouldn't dare approach him, and that's not just because he was famous. If I saw him, I knew I'd better be walking on the other side of the street.

People remember how they put us on the back of the bus, and they forget how they put us on the front of the train. We went to the back of the bus because they were diesels, and those fumes would kill you and the ruling gentry was not going to sit there. During my time as a youngster, trains were fueled with coal, so that car right behind the engine had no air-conditioning, and if they kept the windows closed you'd suffocate, and if they opened them up you'd choke to death. The gentry, they were breathing easy in the last car. That's how they did it. That's how it was. For away games, the white kids would be riding in a nice, warm bus. We'd be in the back of a truck, huddled up with canvas and straw.

Now they tell us, "Forget it, get over it." Someone says, "Earl, are you still angry?" Of course you're angry! It would be disrespectful to ever stop being angry. I saw people lost, people with great potential whose lives were utterly wasted. You remember me. Who remembers them? The question is whether that anger keeps pushing you forward, or whether you let it eat you away. And there are thousands and thousands of kids across America being eaten up by something they don't even understand. They inherit the anger without knowledge of their own history, when their history is the one thing that can get them through the anger. That brings it back to the parents, to the teachers, why they matter so much. Because they've got to serve as the guides for these kids. Somebody has to be there to do it.

We lived it, that whole ball of wax. My parents did their best to keep us safe in the box where we were put. They'd tell you there was no reason for a black kid to be on Mount Vernon Avenue after dark, even if there was a completely legitimate reason. You get me? Because the cops are going to stop you just for being in the neighborhood, and you did not want the cops to stop you. They weren't there to protect us. Once they stopped you, anything could happen.

This is what breaks your heart. The kids today have to learn their own survival tactics, and they're basically trying to protect themselves from kids just like themselves. That's so crazy, because they ought to finally be able to feel safe. During my childhood, you had to know how to approach folks, and how not to approach folks, and to understand the risks if you did it the wrong way. I never saw a cross burning, or someone being dragged out and lynched; we made sure we didn't do anything to incite that kind of violence. But we knew about those things. We knew they could happen. And you spent your childhood making sure you never put yourself in that position.

Today, I try to explain that to kids whenever I speak with them. These kids have to wonder about the fairness of it all, why they're born into poverty, why too many times their dads are gone, why it's so much easier for so many other kids. I tell these kids that I understand. Every minute of our lives, we knew what we didn't have, and how life was so much easier for all those kids on the other side of town. If you could not manage your anger at that unfairness, there were only a few ways to end up: you could be a drunk, or you could be in prison, or you could be dead. None of that has changed. The difference is that we always had a source of hope. It was the great gift from those who loved us the most. Maybe things weren't going to change immediately, but we felt they were going to change in our lifetimes. Hope protected us; hope drove us. But you understood why some people gave up, and once they did they were finished. You still loved them, because you knew what had broken in them. That's what you still see today. The hardest thing, the tragedy, is when that hope is already gone when a child is four, five, six years old.

I went to very small schools, and I felt it from the very beginning. Our teachers understood: if there was going to be any way out, they had to play the pivotal role. I don't know how much the teachers feel it today, but our teachers knew that lives were on the line. In our elementary school and high school, that's the kind of passion they gave us on a routine basis. Teachers, coaches—in my heart, they'll always occupy the highest place, right next to my parents. Every day they'd reassure us, and every day they'd teach us, and every day we'd get on a bus and go right to the "colored section."

From the time I was little, I was always a pretty good student. One of the hardest things that happened to me was when I skipped a grade in elementary school. Even now, I would never recommend that for a kid, because there's a huge difference between a fifth grader and a seventh grader, which is what happened to me: I skipped the sixth grade. I did well academically, but I wasn't ready socially. Oh, man. Those kids were a lot older, a lot more mature. What saved me was the way my teachers looked out for me. They understood. You'd go through those doors every day, those magical portals, and at night you'd come home and see your parents, dead tired from shoveling coal or cleaning someone else's bathroom. They wanted you to be learning. They wanted that for their children. Now, with too many kids, learning is seen as the white man's game, and it just kills me. That's like giving in to everyone who held us down.

The teachers understood what was going on. In our scheme of things, the most important people were doctors, who were there when we needed them—most of the white doctors wouldn't even see us—and then the teachers. Our parents were not educated, and they wanted their children to be educated. Any support our teachers needed from our parents, they got it. No questions asked. Kids today, you hear about all these discipline problems, and then the parents go to school and blame it on the teachers. In my day, you wouldn't dare think about disrupting a class. My parents told me, "You need what your teachers are trying to offer you. And you'd better take it with a smile."

I'm in the Hall of Fame, and people remember me because I played basketball. You want to know who I remember? Helen Day. This woman was a great teacher, and she was also a close friend of my mother's. At first, I was going to listen out of fear, because I knew what would be waiting for me at home if I didn't. But it didn't take long to know there was something magical in that classroom. When Helen Day closed her door and started teaching, the whole world opened up. They named a postal station after her in Alexandria, and even now, when they name a postal station after a black elementary school teacher in that place, that means as much as any plaque in any Hall of Fame. She demonstrated early that she cared about me. I know how hard it is for teachers today, and I know the pressures they're under, but I think so much comes back to that one thing: no matter how strict you are, no matter how tough you are, the kids have to know you care about them.

Once you love a teacher like that, if she told you to go climb a barbed-wire fence, you'd climb it. Helen Day was dynamic, and whatever she said, you were clinging to the words. There was reverence in that classroom. I don't know how it could be like that today. The only way would be if school buildings were filled with adults who saw their teaching jobs as the highest calling in their lives, who completely understood that what they did every day was life or death for these students, and who loved those students as much as their own children. I know many teachers are still that way, but all our teachers were that way. All of them. They came from the same place as us. They knew they'd never make it out, so they gave us all their best hopes. The kids today, all I hope for them is that they have someone they can look back upon in that same way, when they're eighty.

That's our hope. It's not about money or speeches. It's about taking time, the one thing most people don't want to share, and giving it to children who desperately need it, and making sure they know you're giving it from love. Because if you think it's inconvenient, and you begrudge those kids the time, they'll know. Kids always know.

Start with my parents. They were always there for me. But if you were in a conflict at school and asked for help, you'd better be right. My mother always told me she'd support me if I was doing the right thing. My dad would come home tired, eat, take a bath, and go to sleep. My mother didn't sleep, not when it came to us. I came home one day and said, "Miss Day was picking on me," and I know that's how it happens with a lot of kids today: it's never their fault, it's always the teacher's fault. My mother said to me, "You're telling me she walked into that class and started picking on you?" The next question was, "What'd you do to attract Miss Day's attention?" and that was about as far as it got. My mother looked at me, and she knew. She said, "The Miss Days of the world are your ticket out of here, and when you want to say something and she doesn't recognize you, put your hand down and keep your mouth shut."

In high school, another hero was waiting for me in Coach Louis Johnson. He was the right guy, put there for a reason. He coached football, baseball, basketball, and most of us played them all. When you think of why our kids play basketball now instead of baseball, maybe it really does begin back then. There was nothing for us in the summers when I was a kid, and we had no nice facilities to go to play, and there were no jobs for black kids. So we played ball. Basketball was just one of the things I played, but it was easy: one ball and a playground, and everyone could play. But baseball—in those days, I really loved baseball. Basketball was just an easier game when you wanted to get some guys and play.

We'd play touch football in the morning, softball in the early afternoon, and when the sun was about ready to go down we'd play basketball on the playgrounds, with wooden backboards, because no one was going to give us steel or glass. We played in the evening, when it was cooler, and we played real hard. That carried over for us into high school. It seemed like every school we played used a zone, which wasn't bad for us because we had people who could shoot and people who could rebound. Because of our designation, we always played schools that had bigger enrollments, even though we had fewer than three hundred kids in our school.

One game that will stand out for me forever was in football: we played Frederick Douglass out of Baltimore in our homecoming game. Douglass was a much bigger school with much better equipment, and they came in and we dominated them. We gave them a steady diet of Oliver "Bubba" Ellis, a teammate at Parker-Gray who was the best all-around athlete I'd ever seen. They couldn't believe it, but we beat them by three or four touchdowns. That wasn't so unusual; we always did well against the schools from Washington or Baltimore. Later on, Oliver transferred from Howard to West Virginia State, and we were roommates.

In high school, we weren't stupid. We knew what we didn't have. With our uniforms, we brought them home and sewed up everything. The jerseys. The pants. It was a sad state of affairs. You make do, and you channel that anger. You take pride in who you beat. In basketball, I was listed as a center, and I was in the middle of the zone defense. In baseball, I can't even remember losing a game. I pitched and batted fourth. We had a little bandbox of a ballpark, and no one wanted to come in and play us.

I graduated from high school in 1946, the year Jackie got signed by the Dodgers and played his minor league ball. We all knew what was happening. We were all following him. That's what brings me back to how silly it is when people say I was like Jackie Robinson. I don't know if anyone even noticed my first game in Rochester. But in 1947, black kids in America were focused on him. Baseball was the game that mattered for the whole nation, and the Major Leagues—the supposed epitome of the game—were all white. You can't understand how much Jackie meant to us. What I went through and what he went through are totally different. Here's a guy whose own teammates hated him. He faced that every day he walked into the ballpark. I never went through that, not on that level. His only sanctuary was when he went home at night.

You get to this point, and you look back, and I really need to share the truth. If there's a secret to what happened, the secret is this: I owe it to all these people who cared about me. I owe it to Louis Johnson, this coach who was a miracle worker. And I owe it to Helen Day, this wonderful teacher, and all the teachers who cared as much as she did. My worst nightmare was always the fear of letting down the folks who cared about me. You can't do that. You can't disappoint those people. So if you take care of yourself, you're also taking care of the people you don't want to hurt. The kids who say what they do is no one else's business, they don't see. Every child is someone else's business.

I was talking to some of these kids not long ago, and I said to them, "Everyone needs motivation. What motivates you the most?" They said money. I said, "Money? Money's not even close. Fear motivates people. You want money? It's right there in the banks. Why aren't you robbing it, if it's the most important thing?" They say, "Because I don't want to go to jail." So fear is bigger. You've just got to pick the right fear, a beneficial fear, and let it drive you. I feared letting down all these folks who loved me.

Kids today, we've got to change their views on life. The way it is, they're going to go out and have a good time, and they aren't going to care who they hurt while they're doing it because they don't expect to live past thirty. They've got no one they worry about disappointing, because the people who raised them are living the same life. These kids can sense that too many teachers do their jobs and then go home, although these same teachers get worn down by years of teaching kids who have no hope, kids who never learned the value of knowledge. So the only ones who seem to be there for these kids are their friends, and their friends are leading the worst kind of lives, and they're the ones these kids don't want to disappoint. That's a definition for suicide. If you're in that life, the only fear you have is letting down the people standing with you. Once you see those people dying on the corner, there's nothing left. You're not thinking ahead to any 401(k).

When I was a kid, you didn't have those temptations, all that money on the street. There were no two-hundred-dollar sneakers. We wore Converse, the old canvas shoes. These kids, these leather sneakers, they wear them with everything, even when they get dressed up. Even teenagers who get every break in the world need to see that sign on the fridge:

"Leave home now, while you still know everything." You think at that age you're so damn smart, and that's when adults have to stand up. The telephones and all the things they have today—it doesn't make any difference. If the kids are smarter, it's not smarter in the ways that matter. They need to learn discipline, they're hungry for discipline, and I don't use the word to mean punishment. If kids can't learn discipline—and that means helping their families, doing their schoolwork, looking out for neighbors, doing hard work when it's easier to quit—then all those radios and cell phones and computers and TVs are only getting in the way of the real lessons about life. That teenager may be telling you to go to hell, but he's watching you. He's watching everything you do. He's taking notes.

My oldest brother, Ernest, my mother let him quit school, and he did all right for himself. He went into the military, then came home and worked for the Alexandria gas company. My brother Ted finished high school, got drafted, and came back and went to school on the G.I. Bill. He graduated from the Howard University School of Economics, with honors, while he was working at a full-time government job. We lost Ted a few years ago. My whole family is gone, my brothers and my father and mother, and now the baby is going to be eighty-one. I'm the last man standing, and maybe that's why I've got to do this book, because I think they'd all agree with the message. At this stage of life, when I reflect sometimes on all the people I love, all the high school buddies who are gone . . . I've seen a lot of people buried, and a lot of knowledge buried with them.

I was reading somewhere that in the old days, the "Colored only" days of my youth in Alexandria, the average life expectancy for a black guy was sixty-four. So you can say I'm living on borrowed time, and there are some things I really need to say.

I try to take care of myself. I don't drink or smoke. If I enjoy a luxury, it's eating out. I always like eating where it's comfortable. My favorite meal was always smothered pork chops, but now I see the gravy and the fried onions in there and I think: better not. My mother was a country girl—oh, the desserts she could make!—and she always tried to make enough to last. We didn't have much money, but we ate very well. She believed, like country folks do, in a big breakfast. It was nothing for us to sit down and eat pork chops in the morning, because she knew what the dietitians say today: your big meal should be breakfast or lunch, so you can spend the rest of the day burning it off. Those were dastardly times, and you had to learn how to live without spending a lot of money. We weren't angels, but we all got along—no gangs, no serious fights. Out of my friends, I don't recall anyone going to a reformatory.

That's being blessed. At every stop I made in my development, I was in the right place, with the right people. You can't believe how much easier everything can be when every adult in your community seems to have your best interests at heart. A man lives up to the faith of the people who care about him, even if it's just one person. Let those people down, and you're not a man.

My senior year in high school, we enjoyed a lot of success, and it was even more of an accomplishment when you saw what we had to deal with. We didn't have a gymnasium, a baseball field, a track—absolutely nothing. Here we're sitting in Alexandria, eight miles from Washington, capital of the nation, and we had nothing.

Except we had that magical coach, Coach Johnson. His whole demeanor still has an effect on me today. He coached me in baseball and basketball, my favorite sports, and baseball probably had a little edge. But even though I loved it, it didn't have the intensity of basketball, unless you were in a no-hit game or something.

Basketball was intense at all times, and if you wanted to win, you had to maintain that intensity. When my senior year came, in my household, you didn't sit at the dinner table and talk about going to college. My parents knew I was going. They knew I had to do it if I was going to have any chance of living a different life than what they'd lived. They wanted more for their children. I was the first one who was able to go, because of finances. My parents believed that you do better when you know better, and the more you know, the better you do.

In the end, it came down to what Coach Johnson said. He didn't holler. He never screamed. He just had tremendous presence. He taught me early: So much in life comes back to how you carry yourself. If you're angry, make it work for you. Or else it buries you.

I look back on those days, and I am thankful for the love of all those people surrounding me, but I don't forget. For the sake of the kids today, I can't forget. People ask me to come and speak, and I tell them how it is and how it was, and then, all of a sudden, they don't want to hear it. But I say to them, you asked me to speak for a reason. You want our experience. All right. Here it is.

4

A Neighborhood Could Play
with One Ball

People talk about basketball now as black America's game, the black American pastime. You're asking me if somehow I played a role in making that happen. The strange thing is, like I said before, baseball was probably my favorite game. Everyone in those days played baseball. But basketball gave me the chance, and I took it. This scout for Branch Rickey, Rex Bowen, offered me a baseball contract. He wanted me to go to Oklahoma, which was not a place a black kid wanted to be at that time, and there was always the chance I'd be in the minors for ten years.

With basketball, I knew could step right into the big leagues if I made it. That was it. That helped me make my decision. I wasn't thinking of what came next. Now, if you ask me about why all the kids play today, I have a philosophy or belief on how that came to be, and why it stays that way. A big part of it is economics. A whole neighborhood can't use one tennis racket to play a game made for two. And you can't play baseball unless you've got the right equipment and a field big enough to play on. If you don't have a catcher, you're not going to throw fastballs, and no one's playing catcher without a mask and chest protector.

Your options are limited with a lot of sports if you're in the city, but a whole neighborhood can play a whole lot of basketball with one ball and one rim. That's affordability. It costs nothing. Baseball or hockey, they demand all that equipment, and there can be a lot of expense.

That's the biggest reason basketball took off and then became a way of life. That's sociological more than anything. A neighborhood can play with one ball: two teams playing, one guy on the sidelines who says, "I got game." It's an outlet in a place that often doesn't offer many. And we all need an outlet, all of us. For my community—for many, many years—it's been basketball. It costs nothing. You get up, you go to the playground, and you play the game. A lot of people, especially kids, define themselves that way.

Now, I also understand that it's become more than that. I remember doing an interview once at Tennessee Tech, and the guy asked me, "Earl, for black kids today, do they see basketball as their best way out?" And I said, "No." It might become a way out, something they talk about, and what kid wouldn't dream about getting the big contracts? But I think, beyond all else, it's become a social thing, a matter of community. Everyone plays. It brings everyone together.

It's no accident that the Rucker League and the Baker League are flourishing in the heart of New York City and Philadelphia. The guys who run those leagues are miracle makers. They understand the big picture. They understand that basketball is a passion that will bring the kids to them. You can't begin to imagine how many lives those guys have touched. You can't even guess at the number of kids who would have ended up with nothing, going nowhere, but instead got scholarships because someone noticed them playing in those leagues.

The dunking thing, this whole idea that you're defined by the way you play above the rim, came along long after me. In my time, dunking was dangerous. It was considered grandstanding. I never dunked. But I'm not down on it. These kids today are supermen. Even the backcourt people play over the rim. You see a guy five-foot-six, Spud Webb, winning a dunking contest. Everyone dunks.

I still go to basketball games, but I really love to watch the games in my den because you get to see the good players make every play twice, whatever they do. They are so skilled that sometimes you just ask yourself, "Did I just see what I thought I saw?" And then you get the replay, and you see it again.

That's today's game. Flying above the rim and dunking, for me, would have been dangerous, because it would have been seen as showboating. You just might end up in the fourth row of the bleachers.

Today, I can absolutely understand how the dunk electrifies people and brings the crowd into the game. But there's also a danger for today's dunkers, as relating to serious ankle injuries and Achilles tendon injuries and knee injuries.

I saw a tremendous transition in the game, and I played against many, many great players. People ask me now to name my all-time team, the absolute greatest that I played against, and that's a hard challenge. Let me tell you a story. You won't see Wilt Chamberlain's name in here, because I never played against him. But I owe him a debt that I'll explain later. He took a potentially gut-wrenching decision and turned it into a no-brainer.

My list would always have to start with Russ, Bill Russell. Then there was George Mikan, and Elgin Baylor, and Oscar Robertson. There was Bob Pettit. And Paul Arizin. And George Yardley. And Chuck Cooper. And Maurice Stokes, "Big Mo," and Sweetwater Clifton . . . Sweets was always tough. "Cous," Bob Cousy. Dick McGuire. Philly had a guy, Neil Johnston. Rochester had Bobby Davies, and Minneapolis had Jim Pollard, who played with Mikan. Here's some more names: Sam Jones and Don Barksdale of the Celtics. Barksdale was unique because he was the first black player in the NBA to play in an all-star game.

Elgin, he was the toughest guy to guard, period. I'll talk about him elsewhere in this book, but if you're looking for the real pioneer of the game these kids play today, he's the one. More of them should know his name. And Oscar could do everything—everything—well. When God put him on the court, he gave him the total package. George Mikan was a big and powerful man and very, very skilled. In the end, they had to change the rules to beat him. The twenty-four-second clock was good for basketball in general, but the reason guys like Danny and Leo wanted the clock was to beat George Mikan, period. But I'll stick with Elgin and Oscar as my greatest all-around players. Oscar and Elgin—they just epitomize the total physical package.

Russell was on a pedestal, a case unto himself. No one could ever affect an entire game like him. No one. You'd guard him and he'd only score sixteen or seventeen, but what he'd do at the other end could absolutely destroy you. Russ and I are good friends, and we still end up at the same venues from time to time, and I am always just so appreciative of how smart a guy Bill Russell is. He was the same way as a player, and he had great skills, and he had this understanding of how to completely disrupt a game and a team's entire flow. The way I'd describe Russ is with a question: "When one guy can completely undermine your offense, what are you going to do?" When you played the Celtics, you knew there'd be no measurable amount of easy baskets for your team, and in the NBA, the team that gets the most easy baskets wins. It's that simple.

Let me tell you, he changed basketball, because there's never really been anyone else who could do it like he did. He popularized a phase of the game where—until he came along—they hadn't even bothered to keep stats. Today, you watch these guys play, and some guy will block a shot and knock it into the second tier, and the crowd goes crazy, except the other team gets the ball back and then inbounds it and scores anyway. Russ had hands like feathers. Russ didn't block shots. He killed shots and took possession of the ball. He'd block it, and it would land at his feet. You look for consistency as a sign of greatness: in all the years I played against Bill Russell, I never saw him have a bad defensive night. Never.

Maurice Stokes—people forget about him because his career was cut short by a brain injury. But he was a player. Lebron reminds me a little of him. Maurice wasn't as quick, but he could handle it and pass it, and he was six-foot-eight, and he could shoot it. There was George Yardley, very small for a forward but very quick, another guy who could really shoot. These were the guys you were going up against, night after night. The game was rough, and some teams liked to talk—I used to say the Fort Wayne players got two feet taller and a lot louder when they played at home—but there wasn't the kind of trash talking there is today. Sam Jones had this little saying. He'd drop that jump shot of his, and you'd go in to try to block it, and he'd say, "Too late." But that was about it.

I played hard, and I had a few fights, but that was only to make sure you set the proper tone. There were certain things you had to address, like if you went in for a layup and a guy undercut you. You had to address it immediately, because that was the kind of thing that could end a career. For us in particular, in the 1950s, a career in basketball was nothing to take for granted. We knew where we'd be if they took that away from us. So if that guy undercut you, you had to let him know you disapproved, and you did it by touching him up a little. That's how you discourage that kind of activity. If he gives you a low blow, or a blow to the face? Those are no-nos. We had this one play, for instance, that we'd run if their big guy was doing things that had to be addressed. You'd overplay him, and they'd get the ball to him, and if he was any kind of player he'd sense the way you were guarding him, and he'd pick the ball up and turn into you. But when he did, you'd be standing right there. Understand? And he'd come into you in a way that nobody wants to do it. You never want to hurt anybody, but certain things need to be addressed, and if he turns and you're right there, in that way, then he'll remember.

Many of today's players I haven't met. But some of them do understand. I've spoken to Michael Jordan, and he was very appreciative and very generous in the things that he expressed to me. I've met Shaquille O'Neal and LeBron and Allen Iverson. When John Thompson was working with TNT, he came to my house and did an interview where he asked, "Who would you pay to see play?" I told him I'd take one of his kids: Allen Iverson. He's a throwback, tough as nails, and Lord knows he can play at both ends of the floor. Then he asked, "Out of all the guys you've seen, whose career do you respect the most?" I said, "Charles Barkley. Let me tell you, Charles played in the valley of the giants every night. He gave away inches game after game. He played against the giants, and he played against people who could just flat-out play, and he passed both tests: the test of time, and the test of consistency." A couple of nights later, they showed the interview on TNT while Charles was working in the booth, and when they showed it, Charles choked up. Someone said, "Charles, it's not often you have nothing to say!" and he said, "That is, without question, the nicest compliment I've ever had."

But if you ask me for my favorite player, it's Bruce Bowen. He's got the same job I had. Night after night, he guards the toughest player on the floor. He makes life easier for the scorers on his team. All his points are hustle points, and coaches love him, and a lot of kids don't know who he is. But he's a guy who's going to help you win games.

These players today, these young guys, I've got nothing but love for them. I want nothing from them, except for them to try to be the absolute best. When the NBA brings me in to talk to them, I don't talk to them about their playing style, except maybe to praise them. I talk to them about the most basic ethic in life: "It's not how much money you make; it's how much you keep." That's not just about basketball. That's the only way you survive in life. Saving money comes back to the simplest thing, and that's the thing I was given when I was growing up, and it's the thing we have to somehow give to the kids today: once you believe there's no way out, there is no way out. So someone has to be there to help you to believe. Why do you save money? Because you have faith that life doesn't just matter today. It will still matter in five years, and in fifty years. From the time I started school, I had people I believed in, people who loved me, who were telling me there was a way to succeed. I was a black kid born in Virginia in 1928. My prospects were slim and none, and here I am.

Every year the NBA brings me in to talk with the rookies. Some of the kids know who I am, and some of them don't. The first thing I tell them is to always support your players' association. I explain we had no players' association when I played. Consequently, there was no one to go to the wall for us.

I give my talk every year, and I talk about Sweets and Chuck and myself. The kids listen, and one time one of them said to me, "Mr. Lloyd, we really owe you." I told him thanks, but no, you don't owe me anything. The people you owe are the players who'll come up after you. Just be sure, when you're done, you've made it better for them.

5

Cocoon and Butterfly

If you visit my college, West Virginia State, you'll think it's just a little place, a quiet place, an out-of-the-way place. But I cannot tell you enough about what that school means to me, or the sense of peace I feel every time I go back. For me, going there, it was like a butterfly coming out of a cocoon. It was a fabulous place during dastardly times. When I get asked about the most memorable time of my life, I think people always expect me to talk about the championship season in Syracuse. But it was my college career. Without it, I have no idea where I might be today.

That I even made it to college was incredible. Remember, for a black kid in the South in the 1940s, your only option was going to be an all-black college. Even then, it would be a hard thing to get in because of the number of people looking for those spots. For a guy like me, without sports, the chances were slim and none. We had young girls, girls who were so smart it was unbelievable, and they had no chance. They couldn't even dream of a job or getting out. They'd finish high school by seventeen, and they'd marry young men who didn't go to school. By twenty or twenty-one, they had two or three kids, and they were trapped. You look at it today, and too many things are the same, even when they should be different. Drive into any city in this country, and you'll see teenagers pushing baby strollers, and for some reason that makes a lot of folks angry. But it's funny how the angriest people are always the ones looking in from the outside, the ones who've never lived it. I just get sad for the girl, for the baby, for all the could-have-beens, because our whole history in this country is full of could-have-beens.

Too many kids still feel trapped, and make choices that keep them there. What they don't know—what they don't believe—is that they have real options now. That's what breaks your heart, because you know it would break the hearts of all these kids who came before them, the kids in my time who wanted out so badly and couldn't even dream of it. Where were they going anyway, even if they had tried? In a lot of cities, you couldn't get a job picking up garbage. These were people who had the skills to be doctors, researchers, educators—folks who could have changed the world. And that was crushed inside them. Today, when I go to places where they honor me, I think of the ones who didn't have the same opportunities. That's an obligation for as long as I am here, because they have no memorial, no Hall of Fame.

The girl with that baby stroller, things have changed enough so the chance for her exists, if she studies, if she works, if she's given the support. But all too often she's coming up in a place where she doesn't have that support, and she doesn't feel the kind of warmth and love at school that I felt as I came up, and all around her the world seems to be falling apart. Maybe there's no sign saying she can't go here or can't go there, the way it was for me when I was a kid. But soon enough, that child knows the truth. She knows she's got no chance, and she's going to follow the only path she knows.

We didn't have much when I was a kid, and we lived in a dangerous world, but I can't say this enough: all around me, from the time I was small, I was surrounded by people who were hungry for knowledge, black men and women who saw knowledge as our right. I took that with me when I went to college, and I only got that chance because I was an athlete. I appreciated the opportunity, because I saw how much my parents appreciated it. Like I've said, when I was a kid, you wanted to be one of two things: a teacher or a coach. Make it that far, and you'd be a major success. The people in those positions were our towering role models, and in school their approval was really all that mattered to us.

You'd see the white kids go by on the bus, while we walked to school on the side of the road. You'd see the white people in town, with all the good jobs. They'd look you in the face and say, "Separate but equal." That's a joke. You'd have to laugh.

But at college, on that little campus, I was equal. We all were. Our college had to be more than just an institution of higher learning. It had to be a safe house, and most important it had to be a place to belong. You'd ride the bus into that place, and you could see the school's water tower from a long ways off, and you knew you were home and you knew you were safe. I still feel that way today, when I go back there.

In life, all you ever want is for the playing field to be level; you don't want to start a hundred-yard race ninety-eight yards behind, which is how

8. Ready to go at West Virginia State. In college in the late 1940s, Earl was called upon to be more of a scorer, a role he had to relinquish in the NBA. (Courtesy of West Virginia State University)

it was then, and how it is for a lot of these kids today, kids who get blamed for not catching up. All you want in school, just as in sports, is fair play. When I'm out speaking, and I tell folks that from kindergarten to college graduation I never had a white classmate, or even a conversation with a white person who wasn't telling me what to do, they don't believe it. I say, "Believe it." But the playing field leveled out real fast, once I got to college.

People today say, "Give me the period in your life that you treasure the most," and they expect me to say the NBA. Pro basketball had its purpose and it served me well, and no doubt the longer you live, the more famous you get, which is what I'm still learning every day. But the times I treasure were my college years; they were nothing but nurturing.

From 1946 to 1950 West Virginia State gave me a friendly port in a storm. The people at that college gave you such a huge dose of love and nurturing that students cried when they left. They didn't want to leave. Ask anyone who was there, and they'll tell you: it was a magical place.

Maybe that's because we were ten miles away from Charleston [West Virginia], where life was pretty much the same as it was anyplace else. But we could have been a thousand miles away. On campus, there was a feeling like we'd never had in our lives. It was ours. We didn't have to watch out for anyone. We could go wherever we wanted, stand wherever we wanted. We never had to be anyone but ourselves. I'm not sure it's possible for the kids today to appreciate just how sweet that was. But think of it: in Alexandria, if you were on the wrong street at any time, it could get you thrown in jail—or hurt. You lived with that. You lived with the idea that if a crime happened, and they needed a culprit, they were going to find someone to fit the crime. That was gone once I set foot onto the campus at West Virginia State.

Now, once you got there, the seniors put you through what you might call an orientation. A lot of the guys who really ran the show around campus were varsity athletes, and they might say, "Look, take this girl's luggage to her room for her," and if they said that, you were going to do it. Or they might come around and wait until you were sleeping and then scare you half to death, that kind of stuff.

Every college freshman had a job imposed by the seniors. The job was always very difficult, usually impossible, and these guys expected you to do it. The seniors gave me the nickname "Moonfixer," and that became "Moon," and the people who knew me then still call me by that name. I was the tallest freshman on campus. The idea was that these older guys would be taking their girls out on a date, and they wanted some moon-light if they decided to go out for a walk, and my job was to reach up and make sure the moon was shining when they were with their girls. That was my job, and they expected me to come through. They made me the "Moonfixer," and it stuck.

Once we got through all of that, we got down to business. Like I say, a lot of people think the NBA championship had to be my greatest moment, but I don't know if anything can compare to what happened in college. It's like so much else in our history: hardly anyone remembers now, because so much of it's been lost. Twice, we were black-college national champions. My freshmen year, we were 17-4 or something like that. I was a kid, a baby, on that team. A lot of our guys were just coming back from the war, and we had a big, smart, experienced team. It's funny to think how I played a fast-breaking game at Syracuse, where they invented the twenty-four-second clock, because our strategy in college was the exact opposite. Our coach was Mark Cardwell, and he was way ahead of the curve. We were a big

9. With Frank Enty, a former West Virginia State teammate, at a gathering of players from the championship years. (Courtesy of West Virginia State University)

team, and we weren't a running team; we held the ball and ran what basically was a figure-eight offense. If we had you down in the last quarter running that offense, then you were in a lot of trouble. And we never played a zone, always man-to-man, which inadvertently got me ready for the NBA, even though you know I wasn't thinking about the NBA back then.

There was no jamming, no dunking. To our coach, it would have been like showing off. I was lucky, because my coach in high school, Coach Johnson, had played for A. B. Hamblin, the same person who coached Mark Cardwell. Dr. Hamblin was still at school when I was there; he was as famous as a biology professor as he was as a coach. He's in the State of West Virginia's athletic Hall of Fame as a coach. On the West Virginia State University campus, the science building bears his name. I challenge anyone to find me a coach in a Hall of Fame with a science building named after him.

Most kids, when they leave high school, have a whole new set of mores and rules and values to get used to from their coach in college. Not me. My high school coach learned his system from my college coach, who'd learned from Dr. Hamblin. In Alexandria, my parents listened to Coach Johnson, and they were just so pleased I was going to college. When my mother asked where I was going to school, and I said I didn't know, her next question was, "Where did Coach Johnson say?" At that time, with a guy like that, it was like God was speaking. So that's how I ended up at West Virginia State. I made the commitment to my coach, and then I got on the bus and went there. My thing was, if this school could make me half the man that Coach Johnson was, then it's a perfect fit.

I've never had a regret about that choice. Not one. I never really knew much about my grandparents, but I know they didn't go to college, and I know my parents never got the chance. When I left, they weren't thinking about professional basketball, or anything like that. They were thinking that their child would be a college graduate. Now let me ask you: if you get on the bus, and you know you are carrying those kind of expectations from the people you love most in the world, you're telling me you're not going to measure up? That's not an option.

Look, the first place I lived as a child was pretty humble, although I never saw it in that way, and they tore down that place and built projects in its place. We moved into those projects, and we had a nice place with three bedrooms, which to us was really a nice place to live. And then my folks moved to D.C. when I was a sophomore in college.

Now, when I lived in the projects there were no stigmas attached, at least not the kind kids run into today, when people denigrate the folks who come from projects. My point is that everything becomes a step up for somebody, and the projects—for my family—were a big step up, a quantum leap. I won't say my childhood home was a slum, because *slum* has a strange connotation, as if it's about the people who live there as much as the conditions. But looking back on it, my first memories are of what they'd now call substandard housing. That was our life. And the projects were the next step up from that housing.

My parents understood that college was the one way for me to really get out of there. But West Virginia State was a lot more than that. It was a refuge, a sanctuary. When we traveled as a team, we stayed right on the campus of the team we were playing, because no one in any nearby town was going to let us stay at their hotels. The most important thing, as always, was that the right people were there to see us through it. My success in basketball began with this: my college coach and my high school coach were teammates who played for the same guy. I got the message from them early: try to be half the man Dr. Hamblin was. They learned under him, and they taught me, and then I went to West Virginia State and sat in the classroom of this man who was their hero. I thought I'd be one of his boys. Professor Hamblin let me know very quickly that just because I played basketball, I would not get any special treatment.

It was one more person who had expectations, one more person I needed to please, not only with the books but on the basketball court. You hear all these things nowadays about players having trouble with their coaches. I tell these kids, "A coach is not always right, but never forget he's the one who decides who sits and who plays." So you've got to think about the way you want to express things. How can you be a ballplayer and expect to succeed if you're at odds with the guy who decides if you play? Once you get that reputation, you'll be moving from team to team—I don't care how good you are.

The one game that really stands out for me is the opener in my sophomore year, 1947–48, which was our big season. We knew we were supposed to be pretty good, but Tuskegee came into our gym for the first game ready to go, and we almost blew it. That Tuskegee team was ready; they'd already played two or three games, and we knew nothing about them. It wasn't like today, where you'd be looking at film to learn about a team. It went into overtime, and we hunkered down at the end and held them off by a point. They worked the ball around for a last shot, and I remember that ball hanging up there forever. It hit the rim and came off, and we thought, "Oh, man, are we lucky." If we'd played another minute, we might not have won it.

That was it. I don't know if anyone came close to us again. The whole school would come and just fill that little gym. When I walked into that gymnasium, after the little auditorium where I played in high school, I

10. The undefeated 1947–48 West Virginia State Yellow Jackets. Earl is third from the right, Bob Wilson third from the left. After a close first game, they were never really challenged again on their way to what was known as the "black" national championship. (Courtesy of West Virginia State University)

felt like I was in Madison Square Garden. But in one way, it was like high school: people who had very little to cheer about in life would come out and cheer for us, and we felt that every time we went out on the court. We didn't lose again for the rest of that year, and then we went down and won the Colored Intercollegiate Athletic Conference tournament in Washington, and we were ranked as the black-college champions of the nation. I don't even know who the "white" champions were that year, but I know there was no way they were going to play us. We played in this tiny little bandbox of a gym, and here's something that will tell you all you need to know about the way things work: almost sixty years later, the basketball team at West Virginia State is still playing in that same tiny gym. You look around at these beautiful arenas built for all these other schools, and you ask, "How is that?"

That said, I can't look back on those days and be angry. I played with some fabulous talent at West Virginia State, particularly Bob Wilson, a great player who also made it to the NBA. All the years I played, I don't think I saw him play an off game. The only thing he was better at than basketball was being a decent human being. The guy put us on his shoulders and took us wherever he wanted us to go. I loved him. I have a feeling, when we depart this earth, we'll be hanging around together again.

At college, we felt free from what we'd known all our lives, even if it the reality was never far away. When we traveled, we'd have to make regular stops in the fields or in the woods, because no restaurant was going to serve us, much less let us use their restrooms. For meals, we'd have a big breakfast at the dining hall before we left our campus. Then we'd stop at a store and we'd buy bread and lunch meat and cookies and pop, and we'd have a feast on the hood of the car for lunch. That would hold us until we got to the campus where we were going to play. That school would house us and feed us, because we couldn't stay anyplace else. Crazy, right? But that's how it was.

Coach Cardwell didn't accept the nonsense of those times. West Virginia was a border state; go a little north, and you're in Pennsylvania, and things weren't quite as bad around our college as they had been in Alexandria. In West Virginia, we could ride in the front of the bus, although it ended as soon as you passed any border to the south. I've told you about

11. Earl with former West Virginia State teammate Bob Wilson, during a 2008 ceremony in which Wilson was honored at the school. Close friends, they both went on from college to play in the NBA. (Courtesy of the *Post-Standard*)

the time when we were getting on a bus to go into North Carolina, and the driver—one of these guys in sunglasses and an Eisenhower jacket—said to the coach, "Tell your boys to get to the back of the bus." Coach Cardwell said no, we could ride in the front, and we saw the driver reaching toward a bulge in his jacket, and I'll tell you, we headed for the very back, for the bumper; we knew how this thing could end. Coach Cardwell wouldn't back down. He asked this driver for his name and his badge number, and the driver was just getting madder and madder, and in the end we sat in the back, but Coach Cardwell never forgot. When he came home, he went out and got a couple of eight-passenger DeSoto touring cars to take us to our games. He wouldn't tolerate seeing us treated that way.

I bring that perspective to everything I see today. I watch a lot of news on television, and I was watching one day when a white woman on one of these shows says to someone, I think maybe it was Whoopi Goldberg, "I don't understand. Why is it that we can't use the N word, but it's all right for you to use it when you're talking to each other?" Whoopi tried to explain, but it's something you can't explain if you don't understand: you either know or you don't. It made me think of everything I'd been through, and all the times I heard the word *nigger* used in the worst way, used by experts, and that's exactly why we can use it with each other. I personally feel, if I use that word, I've earned the right to use it. But I'm pleased that word got a good Christian burial.

If you've got to ask why, it's like asking why we get so upset about the Confederate flag being flown over any American city. If you don't understand what that flag means to millions of people whose families were brutalized and torn apart, then you'll never understand no matter how much I tell you. That's the most hopeless kind of kitchen-table stuff. Anyone with any sense of history knows: that flag should never be flown in the United States at any time.

If there's another thing that stands out for me in college, it's our trip west. I guess, more than anything, that trip was evidence of the way things were changing. During my sophomore year, there was actually talk that maybe we'd be invited to the NIT in New York, which at the time was as big as the NCAA tournament today. It never happened. There were teams like Kentucky there, and I guess they weren't going to allow it. But there was this promoter, a guy named Walsh, and he came to Coach Cardwell and asked if we'd be interested in going west, out to California, to play some of the best white college teams they had. We knew what that meant, and so did everyone at the school. Those things didn't happen.

There were about two thousand people who showed up to see us off. None of these other kids had much of anything, but they raised money to give us a little to spend out there. I'll say it again: how could you do anything but your best for people who cared about you that much? This was in 1948, only a year after Jackie broke in with the Dodgers, and you could feel something in the wind. There was this sense of hope.

We went out to the Cow Palace, and it's my belief that we were the first all-black college team to play a white team in that arena. We played St. Mary's in our first game, and they beat us, ending our long winning streak. Maybe everyone figured that showed we weren't for real, but it had the opposite effect on us. We'd traveled cross-country, and we had to play in a strange gym, and we played straight-up against white guys, in front of a big white crowd. How should I say this? We needed that loss to get acclimated. The next game, we beat Santa Clara, and I think that sent the message: we could play with these guys. I think we lost two more close ones when we were out there, but we came back feeling good about ourselves.

My other big memory of the trip is going into San Quentin to play against the prisoners. I don't remember who set that up, but we'd all seen San Quentin in the movies. The prisoners came to watch the game, and they had plenty to say. I remember they had a big guy who went to jump center for the tip, and he looks over at us and says, "You better not out-jump me. I'm in here for murder." Maybe he was putting us on, maybe not. Seems to me that he won the tip.

I can hardly talk about college without choking up. It was a sanctuary, and I still get that feeling when I go back today. In every way, West Virginia State prepared me for what came afterward. Even that trip out west only reminded me of the most important lesson of my life in basketball, the lesson I really learned at West Virginia State, the whole reason we're even sitting down to do this book: once they throw you together on the court, the game ceases to be black or white.

6

The Beginning

The people who tell me I was first—that's a nice thing to say, but I always defer. I make a point of reminding them of Chuck Cooper. He was drafted in the second round in 1950. That's amazing. Without that happening, I cannot conceive of the Washington Capitols picking me seven rounds later. They took me in the ninth round, and trust me, they could have drafted me in the forty-fifth round if there were forty-five rounds, and no one else would have touched me. It was a safe pick.

I live in the Bible Belt, and in the Bible Belt the word *blessed* gets thrown around a lot, even by the heathens, but in this case, absolutely, I was truly blessed. You don't think I remember every guy who came before me, every guy who could play the game and never got the chance in the NBA? We're doing this book because I was blessed in that way, and we're doing it to make sure no one forgets just how many people like me deserved the same break and didn't get it.

Now it's 2008, and no one says their names. I don't forget. You can never forget. Every honor I get, every speech I make, I think of them.

In 1950, and this goes without saying, there were not a lot of options for black folks. I'm sure there were people in my college graduating class who did not get the opportunities they should have had. But there were many people in my class who went to major cities and became executives and military officers and school administrators, and I think what they accomplished is as remarkable, maybe more remarkable, as what happened to me.

I'll tell you this: I had no idea I was going to be drafted into the NBA. My plan was to get my diploma and to be a teacher and a coach, because I saw those jobs as important. Professional basketball? It wasn't even in my mind. I never saw it as a way out. I knew about the Globetrotters and the old Rens from New York, all-black teams that were as good as any in the world, and that was about it. One day, in my senior year, I'm walking across campus and a classmate calls out, "Moon! I just heard your name on the radio!" Now, we never got any coverage at West Virginia State— even when we won the black-college championship, all they gave us with this tiny little article in the Charleston paper—and I asked what she had heard. I was on the radio? She said, "You've been drafted to play for some pro team called the Washington Capitols."

And that was it. I knew I was going to give it a shot. You just couldn't pass up the opportunity. Coach Cardwell called me in to say they wanted me in Washington, and remember I still didn't have my degree. I had planned on staying around to get it, because I was in no hurry to leave college. The dean of the college, Dr. Harrison Ferrell, made me promise I'd come back to get it. And I did, maybe four or five years later. Like I say, my plans had been to get out, teach in a high school, get some experience, and down the road maybe coach in college.

But when my coach told me to go to the tryouts, it was like Jesus Christ himself had told me. The Capitols called him, and they sent him a train ticket to get me to Washington. And I was going. I told my mother, and she was pleased to know about this chance for her baby child, but she said to me, "Just make sure they see your best."

The organization of an NBA team wasn't big then. It was an owner, a publicity guy, a coach, maybe a general manager. Bones McKinney, the coach, he was the only real basketball guy in the organization. He's the one who'd seen me, when we played our college tournament in their building. I've wondered sometimes what it was that caused him to take a chance on me.

Bones, they called him, but his real name was Horace McKinney. He went to Wake Forest, and he came up in North Carolina, and it was 1950 when we met. Think of that. Think of what he'd heard throughout his life, and then think of the way he treated me. It's proof. You can rise above the things you heard when you were small. Bones is gone now. But not too long ago, before he died, we were going through Hickory, North Carolina, where he lived, and we decided we had to stop and call him. His wife answered the phone, and she said to me, "I remember you, Earl. You were one of his favorites." You'd think she was just saying that, but let me tell you a story. We were on the road once with Washington, playing in Indiana, and we checked into a hotel where they allowed me to sleep but wouldn't allow me to eat in the restaurant. So I called for room service. Not long after that, there's a knock on the door, and it's Bones. He says to me, "You're not going to eat by yourself." I told him, "Don't worry, just go ahead," because it's like I was saying, you get to be an automaton; you're used to all of this.

Here's a situation where he'd never have been criticized if he never came to my door. That's a true stand-up guy. I always think of moments like that when anyone wonders why I'm not full of hate. Bones was a decent guy but a tough, two-fisted guy, you know? That time when I called him, he told me he'd become an ordained minister. The last thing I said to him was, "If you're ordained, then there's hope for us all." One of the few regrets I have about the game is that I didn't get the chance to play for a few years with Bones.

People today ask me if I planned a career in the NBA. Are you kidding? How can you plan a career in an arena where you really had no one before you? Chuck, Sweets, myself . . . we became the predecessors. There was one other black guy in my camp, Harold Hunter. I played against him for four years in the CIAA; he was a guard with North Carolina College, and he was also drafted by the Capitols, but he didn't make it through camp.

I think it was because he was a guard, and that's one of the things we were up against. You remember, with the NFL, the whole quarterback stigma that lasted for so long—you know, our guys can't play that position because they can't think, they can't lead, they can't handle pressure, all that stuff, which means generations of great black quarterbacks didn't get a chance because of foolishness, stupidity. We ran into some of the same thinking. During my time, nobody said it, but it was whispered about how most of the black guys who made it early in the NBA were big, physical guys who weren't expected to be cerebral. They let white guys run the team on the floor, and they sent the black guys under the hoop to do the heavy labor, which fit the pattern in this country for a long, long time.

Then guys like Oscar Robertson came in, and Lenny Wilkens, and Hal Greer, and they took care of those whispers. They were guards who took over their teams, and that influx broke all that stuff on the rocks. But Harold Hunter, his time hadn't come, and he was gone. The key to making a team is doing well at what the team needs you to do, or at least at what the coach wants you to do, and that's why you're picked. Harold Hunter had that going against him; things had shifted just enough that they thought I could come in and play defense and rebound. But for Harold, it wasn't going to work.

I don't even know why they drafted him, why they got his hopes up, with the racial climate the way it was in Washington, D.C. That climate was not going to allow the Capitols to stand up and have two black players on one team, taking two jobs away from white guys. Incredible, right? Can you imagine that when you look at the league today? But that's how Harold Hunter lost out. Ask me about being first. I'll tell you about Harold Hunter.

It is so difficult to explain how impossible it seemed to be in that camp at all. If we had any dream as college kids, it was to play for the Globetrotters, who were always looking for the best black college players. In my senior year, once my eligibility was used up, I had a chance to travel with them for a while. For a wide-eyed kid, I'll tell you, those were some exciting times. I remember being in Kansas with them, and they played two games in one day, games that were two hundred miles apart. You imagine?

Goose Tatum was on that team, and then there was Marques Haynes, a great guy whose talents were way ahead of his time. He gets remembered as a showman and as the greatest dribbler ever, but he could flat-out play. He finished college a few years before I traveled with the Globies, and the NBA didn't even get under way until 1949, so think of this: think how we'd remember him today if he was born six or seven years later. Maybe you'd be writing this book about him. Abe Saperstein, the guy who ran the Globies, really felt as if he should have the first shot at all the black players. I remember when I went on tour with them: Mark Cardwell, my college coach, said, "Do not sign anything. Don't sign a dinner check. Forget signing a contract." And I listened.

They did finally offer me a contract, and I didn't sign, but I think Abe figured it was a matter of time and I'd be back. Don't forget, the pro leagues weren't signing blacks at that moment. So when the draft came along and I signed with the Caps, Abe was outraged. He accused the Capitols of stealing one of his players. That was his attitude. He just thought the best black players ought to be with him, with the Globetrotters, who had all these players who couldn't get into the NBA. For Abe, they were entertainers, but no one should ever doubt how great they were.

Years later, in Syracuse, I met a woman named Lottie Graves. They called her "Lottie the Body," and she had a lot of class. She became famous all around the country as an exotic dancer, and she ended up in Detroit at the same time I was in Detroit. I think of her now because she married Goose Tatum, who met her in Syracuse. That's how it worked: even in a town like Syracuse, you could be famous and go there to play ball or entertain, but after the game or the show you couldn't get a drink in a white nightclub. So you'd go out in the Fifteenth Ward, where we basically had to live, and everybody met everybody. And everybody knew about Lottie's dancing.

Lottie was all class, and people would say, "How can you have class and be an exotic dancer?" You had to see her to understand. You had to be in the intimacy of a small club and watch her perform to understand how beautiful it was. But people who never saw her will always talk down and condemn what they don't understand.

That was the climate when I was drafted by Washington. It sounds shocking today that they wouldn't consider letting a black guy run the offense, but that was the attitude. They hadn't been considering black guys, period. I was still surprised when I made the final roster. If they're not going to let two black guys on the team, it was surprising they'd bother to let even one guy on. And that was in our nation's capital, not sixty years ago. How sad a commentary is that? A long way from those days to Barack Obama.

At the time, before Harold got cut, it was like, two black guys on a team? In D.C.? That wasn't just surprising; that was fantasy. My family lived in Washington then, and during the time we were in training camp, Harold Hunter stayed with my mother and myself. I don't remember exactly when he was cut, but he was cut. And I made it. And I still remember. I played up front and he played guard, when a black guy was not going to play guard in the NBA.

I often ask myself why they bothered to pick me, but I know this: I was cheap. Washington didn't need to spend a quarter to scout me. Our conference tournament was played in Washington, in their building. I was a six-foot-six legitimate power forward, and I had a good college career, and obviously they liked something they saw. Bones was the kind of man who might have told them to take the chance.

I'm glad Washington did it, but I know what really gave me the chance—and this is why I'll never have a bad word to say about Red Auerbach, who was running the Celtics at the time—it was Chuck Cooper. I love him, and I still owe him. Just a fabulous person. He was drafted by the Celtics in the second round that year, just unbelievable for 1950, because the Celtics wanted him so badly. But think about this: they could have waited. The chances are, no one would have touched him. There were no black players in the NBA, and someone had to have the courage to take the chance, and Red could have waited and done it in one of the last rounds. Instead, he took him in the second round, and that made it all right for some other teams to take their own little steps, and that may be the only reason I got my chance. I'll always appreciate Red Auerbach and Walter Brown, who owned the Celtics, for drafting Chuck and for all the guys they brought into Boston.

As for the Washington Capitols, they were in no hurry to get to me. I was picked in the ninth round, and I think maybe Auerbach gave them the courage. They knew I wasn't going anywhere. The funny thing is, you see today how the kids gather in New York or around the television to watch the NBA draft. I was back at West Virginia State. I didn't even know it was going on. I wouldn't have believed I would even get considered in that world.

You'd probably be hard-pressed to find a lot of ninth-round draft choices who make it in the NBA, and I will submit this to you, especially when you talk about Jackie Robinson and what it meant when I made the league: after I got drafted, nobody in Washington brought me in to tell me the obvious. You'd think someone might say, "You're the first black guy we drafted, and you've got to do this or you've got to do that if you want to make the team." We all know the story about how Branch Rickey brought Jackie into a room and put him through the whole ordeal, insulted him, insulted his family, told him this is what you're going to hear: can you take it? I was from Alexandria, so they probably figured I just knew. Didn't need to be said. They paid me, I think, maybe forty-five hundred dollars. That was the low end of the scale, but when you're drafting a black kid number nine, what kind of money was I going to command?

I had no illusions. If anything, I was stunned. You have to be honest with yourself, you really do, when you're born and raised in a situation where you're treated like you're second class, third class, fourth class—if that. It creeps in. When you're treated like that, it says to you, "You're inferior," so you're hardly expecting any kind of break. The first question I asked myself was, "Do I really belong here?" I'd never even been in a locker room with white guys before, and now I'm in a training camp with Dick Schnittker of Ohio State, and Bill Sharman, an All-American from Southern California, and Alan Sawyer, an All–Pacific Coast Conference player, and a player named Tommy O'Keefe from Georgetown. I was still wondering how I'd do when I stepped onto the court.

Maybe it's a testament to the kind of guys they drafted, but race was never an issue. We trained every day, we did our routines, our scrimmages, and what happened early on . . . I looked at the quality of the guys I was playing against, and I remembered the quality of the guys I'd played against in college, and I asked myself if I belonged. The answer, very quickly, became yes.

I've been asked, of all the players from those days, if there was one I admire most. Let me tell you, it was Bill Sharman, a great player who'd later coach the great Laker teams with Wilt and Jerry West. He was my friend, and think of what that meant at the time. Of course, when that Washington team folded, he'd end up in Boston and I'd be in Syracuse, and we were fierce competitors on teams that were fierce rivals. But the respect never went away. To this day, we're glad when we get the chance to see each other.

Remember, Washington was in the South in the back-of-the-bus days. Here's a guy, when he found out I didn't have an automobile and was riding the bus to camp, who told me he would pick me up every day at Georgia Avenue and Columbia Road in Washington. And he did. When you spend that much time with a guy, when he's picking you up every day and dropping you off every day, you get to know him pretty well. In all our conversations, race never came up. Never. If he heard anything from anyone else about giving me those rides, he never said a word, and I know what it must have meant when everyone else saw the two of us arriving together. Bill Sharman, to this day I see him and his wife at the Hall of Fame induction every year, and he truly is—and will always be—a class act.

I can't tell you what it was like, just to walk into the locker room at American University and see this wall of white guys. I'd never had a real conversation with a white person of my own age in my life. I didn't act like a different person around them, although for a while I might have been quieter. You try to act the way you were taught, and my parents and my coaches had always reassured me about my worth as a person. And I also knew, if I was going to compete with these guys, that you can't be just as good. To get somebody's attention, you've got to be even better. I accepted that, it became my mantra, and it drove me.

It was the same with the way I carried myself off the court. I always dressed my best; I'm still like that today. Always, in Washington and Syracuse, I wore a shirt and tie. A teammate asked me once, "Why are you always in a tie?" and I said to him, "Remember we went to that nightclub in Fort Wayne, where the sign said, 'We reserve the right to refuse service to anyone who is boisterous or is not properly attired'?" He said, "Sure," and I said, "Who do you think the sign was for? Not you. You can come in butt-naked, and they'll call you eccentric; you'll be fine. I come in without a necktie, and believe me, I'm not properly attired."

I was not going to give them the easy opportunity to send me away. Not on the court, or away from it. I would never wish those conditions on any of the kids today, but I think if they understood what it was like, if they felt it, it might change the way they act when they're in the spotlight. Because that's how it was for me, and for all of us. The ruling gentry was just looking for a reason to say it wouldn't work, we weren't up to it, to send us away, like they'd sent away entire generations before us. Being aware of that helped me get through camp.

Let me put it this way: You hear people talking about pressure, and we understood pressure. For us, it was outside the arena. Inside was the easy part. We knew that we could play.

7

Decisions

Whenever I hear criticism of kids leaving high school and going straight to the NBA, it's almost always from white people, and they're mad because they see a lot of black kids without degrees making a lot of money. The first thing that pops out of people's mouths: "Don't you think they're overpaid?" They say it like a question, but it's a statement.

But we've all been taught the same thing in this society, and we were taught it by the ruling gentry: a fair salary is what the market will bear. So don't get mad at the players. Get mad at the owners.

These kids are teenagers, and they're coming out of situations where there are generations of people who have never had much money. Now they've got a chance to change everything, and they're supposed to pass that up . . . exactly why? These kids, one fall, one bent knee, and their careers are shot, and no one is going to take care of all the people they wanted to care for. If an owner falls down and hurts his knee, you think they take away his team? Or send him back to the projects? These kids are being American: they're getting what they can get while they can get it. Sure, some kids should leave school, and some should not. It's common sense. But for a lot of these kids with real skills, it's a once-in-a-lifetime opportunity. You've got a kid about to make five million, who can make more with one contract than most of us make in a career, and you're saying he should pass it up? When the whole idea of college is to find a better way to make a living? Are you kidding? Of course that kid should leave school! Go ahead and leave!

Why do we send our kids to school? To graduate and do what? Make money at an honest career! We only send them because we've learned folks with college degrees make more than those without a diploma, and those with high school diplomas make more than dropouts. Tell me, how many Ph.D.'s make ten million dollars? Some. Maybe. Few and far between. Now here's some kid from the South Side of Chicago, raised by his mother, who can step out of school and change his family's life. What does he do? Take a look at the first thing all these kids do. The first thing they do, once they sign, is to buy their mother a new home.

I stayed four years in college, sure, but nobody was offering me ten million dollars. The question isn't whether players who can do it should take the contracts and leave early. Of course they should. The question is what the other kids—the ones without that chance—should emulate.

I was talking to a group of kids one day, and a kid who stands maybe five-foot-one tells me he's going to be an NBA player when he gets older. If that's what he wants to dream, fine. All kids dream. The question is if he can handle the disappointment part of it as he gets older, and he learns it isn't going to happen. The difference, maybe, is that when the dream dies for the white kid, he looks around and sees a lot of guys in his life who are very happy, very successful, working at everyday jobs. And the kid I was talking with, he sees the guys in the NBA on his television, and then he looks around his neighborhood, and who does he emulate? Who are the guys he sees? Who are the guys with money? That's a problem. There's a problem to address. He needs more than the NBA dream. He needs a bigger dream to help him graduate. And that dream has to come from people around him.

What's going to be is going to be, with any class in college. People say to me that a lot of these kids who leave early aren't ready for the money. I say, pick any college and eliminate the athletes. Track any class from freshman day through year four. You're always going to lose kids who aren't ready, athletes or not. For some kids, college isn't right. College can be overrated. If I've got a son, a seven-footer with great talent, should he stay in school if he gets offered a big contract? If you say stay, I say why? You say, "Take the education." I say, "What about the mattress full of money?" The last part of the equation: do you have an aversion to that young man going back to college someday as a rich man? That's doable! I went back and got my degree, and to say these kids won't do it assumes exactly what? Young kids in poverty see what other people have, and they want

12. Speaking to the West Virginia State basketball team in 2008: "People have died—been hung or burned or thrown in lakes—for you to have that right," Earl told the players, while urging them to exercise their right to vote. (Courtesy of West Virginia State University)

it, too. When an avenue presents itself so they can get it, of course they're going to listen.

Now if it's the wrong offer, if it's something coming from someone on the street, they're very vulnerable. These kids are not worried about longevity, not on the street, not in the gym. How can you blame them? What do they see? What do they hear? They see poverty, and they see death. So here's the tough thing: I lived in a hard part of town, but there were no gangs. We got support from the adults, who were as poor as we were, and who defined their own success by whether they did enough to help us to make it out. A lot of these kids today, the adults around them are absent or overwhelmed, and these children are beset by gangs. A lot of these kids, just little kids, will get beat up if they won't join a gang, and anyone who says they should just stay strong doesn't know what it means to really get beaten up, and to know you'll probably get beaten up again tomorrow by guys who can kill you if they feel like it. Maybe there's no dad to ask for help, no place to go. This is a little child being recruited for a gang, and there are no resources to help. Can he ask his mother to help, his mother who's working some night job at a hotel or a hospital? And even if she can help, what can she do? Walk every step of the way to school with him? Sit with him in class? Follow him to the bathroom? And even if she could do all of that, do you really think she could scare away these guys in gangs?

That's the difference between what we had and what these kids don't have. People say things were worse during segregation, and in some ways they were. But that whole tier of adult community support is just gone. Every night I sit and listen to Lou Dobbs, and he talks all the time about the "war on the middle class," but I never hear him speak about a war on poverty.

Let me tell you, we live in the greatest country in the world, a country that spends billions and billions to fix problems in Iraq or to fix the problems of some bankers on Wall Street—the kind of guys, like I always say, who own the teams. But in the greatest country in the world, we can't protect that little kid who's getting beaten up by a gang. No, we tell that kid to fix the problem himself, and we mock him and mock his mother when they can't. You judge a country the same way you judge a person: by how it treats those who are less fortunate, those in dire need. I've got to tell you, we're not getting good grades. Here's some advice: Don't be poor in this country. Worse, don't be poor and old in this country. Who speaks for the poor people in this country? Really speaks for them? Who really speaks for that little kid? You wonder why I'm voting for Obama?

People talk about trickle-down theories. Drive through the middle of Detroit, or Syracuse, for that matter. Nothing trickles down to the very poor. Nothing. They're there. They're staying there. You want proof, look at one thing: Katrina. When that tsunami hit Indonesia, help was there in two days. Now here's people in Louisiana, our people, my people, dying on the pavement, dying in the water, and they say race didn't play a part! Race always plays a part! I'd ask those people, especially those in what I call the ruling gentry, what they felt when they saw those people. Was it love? Or was it disgust? Because they did not react like people who felt love.

We've got this problem here, and it keeps growing, and a lot of people take their money and their things and hide as far away from that problem as they can, and if they look back it's just to say, "They should help themselves!" I'd ask, how? How should they have done that in New Orleans? How could those people in the sun on the roofs of their houses, afraid of drowning in water filled with human filth, with bodies—bloated bodies—floating around them, how could they help themselves in that situation? But it's all in what we find important. And I look at the makeup of the people in the Ninth Ward of New Orleans, and I suggest, if those people were white, we'd have seen a different take on their importance. I think we would have been there a lot faster. You don't have to be a Rhodes scholar to figure that out.

It's amazing, man. It's 2008, and we're still talking about this. I go back to Ruby Bridges, that little six-year-old girl, and the armed marshals who had to escort her into school every day, and the adults who stood around, making threats, threatening her life. That little child threatened no one, and nothing, except a way of life. Some of those adults are still alive, and their children grew up getting the same message across the dinner table. Maybe the words are different, but the message is the same, the same message about our worth as a people. It's still there. It poisons the children who hear it, the same way it poisoned generations before them. It hasn't gone away, and it works almost as well as saying "Colored only," but we don't want to address it.

Today, these kids in the cities, they're not legally segregated, but people fear them and hate them without knowing them just as much as they hated Ruby Bridges, without knowing her. You talk about me, and this ceiling I'm supposed to be so proud of busting through, but tell me, aren't we still pouring that cement? Maybe we've found an even better way to do it, because these kids have no access to the kind of adults who got me out, which means their segregation may be even worse and more hopeless than mine was.

People talk about how much things have changed. Please. Don't even go to that place with me. Even some of the people—not all, but some—who cheer Obama to my face, I know what they'll do once they're inside that booth. They will not be able to vote for him because he's black, and they fear the same thing they feared in Ruby Bridges.

Right now, somewhere, there is a little kid all alone who will get beaten up if he doesn't join a gang, and he has no one to ask for help: not

13. Earl in "The Pit," the West Virginia State gymnasium, where the school honored him by hanging a replica of his old jersey on the wall. (Courtesy of West Virginia State University)

the cops, not his father, not his mother, not the teacher who gets into her SUV and drives to a house thirty miles away from the school where she goes every day to teach.

Sometimes, once in a while, that kid somehow survives. Maybe he grows up to be the kid with the choice between taking millions upon millions of dollars or maybe losing everything if he doesn't. You say he should stay in college? He knows what he has to do.

8

Timing

My time in Washington ended when the U.S. Army "deemed me neces-
sary," and I received my selective service notice. That would take me into
my years in Syracuse, although I didn't know it at the time. I got drafted to
go into the army, and I had to leave the team, and I didn't know what would
happen when I came back. While I was in the army, the Caps folded. The
league put all our players into a supplemental draft. Fred Scolari, one of
my teammates, was chosen by the Syracuse Nationals. He recommended
me to the Syracuse management.

Think of that. Think how easily I could have been out of the game.
Scolari had played a big role with the Capitols, and if the NBA holds the
supplemental draft and nobody picks me, I'm gone, hoping to coach at
some little high school someplace. But Scolari made a point of speaking
up for me. He was the career high scorer for Washington, and he went out
of his way to help a black guy nobody knew about in 1950. It just reminds
you about the importance of the way you carry yourself in life, because
you never know who you're impressing, and what difference it can make.
You never know.

Freddy said to Danny Biasone and Leo Ferris, the guys who ran the
team in Syracuse, "There's this kid down there no one is going to pick; you
can pick him up, and you'll get him for a song." That was it. No scouts, no
nothing. I don't think I ever got the chance to thank Freddy. But Syracuse,
for me, was definitely the right place at the right time, and my teammates
were definitely the right people.

Before any of that happened, I did my time in the service. Nothing
really changed. The army had all the same rules I lived with while growing up: we had all-black troops and all-white officers. I spent six months

in Fort Bragg, and I never went into Fayetteville, where they still had the slave-trading blocks in the middle of town. Believe me, that wasn't for tourists or education. If anything, for those folks, it was nostalgia. Then we went to Fort Sill, Oklahoma, and Oklahoma was just a terrible place if you were black. The city bus would come on base, and you could sit anywhere you wanted as long as you were in uniform and the bus stayed on the base, but the instant it left the gates you went to the back of the bus.

That always got to me, because you were wearing the uniform of your country, and some guys were dying in that uniform in Korea. Guys I went to school with came through Fort Sill and went straight to Korea, where they'd have some of the dirtiest, most dangerous jobs in the artillery: the forward observer. But these guys were humiliated, treated as less than human, in uniform in Oklahoma. You don't really think of the West in connection with the worst of segregation, but I swore when I left that state I'd never go back. That feeling had something to do with why I didn't end up in baseball: the Pirates, when they looked at me, wanted me to go to an Oklahoma farm club.

My company commander, Captain Westfall, was a white guy who graduated from West Point. He was a hell of an officer. One morning at reveille, he said the battalion basketball team was not doing so well and inquired as to whether any of us played the game. So I started playing for the camp. We'd travel around to different places in that area and play; there was a team from the Brooke Army Medical Center—they were perennial champions—and we beat them.

In 1950 a lot of guys out of college got drafted right into the army, and there were guys in those games who could really play. I played against Carl Braun and Charlie Shoptaw . . . man, could he shoot it. Our whole battalion would come down to the gym to watch, these guys who had to sit in the back of the bus, guys who couldn't do anything in any of those Oklahoma towns. For them, we turned into their Joe Louis: they knew they were being put upon, and when we played those white teams, they expected us to wear them down and put them out. The guys in the stands expected us to strike a blow for them, because how degraded can you be? We were being asked to be ready to go and die for our country, but over here—even in uniform—you were going to treat us like that?

14. The professional: with his military career behind him, Earl joined the Syracuse Nationals in 1952. (Courtesy of NBA Photos/Getty Images)

I know some people are going to read all this and be surprised at my anger, but I spent my life handling the anger, working through it—which is very different from getting over it. How are you ever going to get over something like that?

I got out of the service and went to Syracuse; two days later, I was ready to play against the Milwaukee Hawks. I can remember some hard things about Syracuse, but I remember beautiful things about living there, too. It was the right fit for me. The right people were there, both professionally and in the Fifteenth Ward, the neighborhood where the black folks in Syracuse basically had to live. I remember trying to rent apartments around town, and people would be fine to you when you were on the phone, and then you'd get there and they'd take one look and they'd say, "Sorry. We just rented it out." Once that happens enough, you know the score.

We had some talent in Syracuse. Dolph Schayes, one of the great scorers in the history of the game, was there. The owner was Danny Biasone, and the general manager was Leo Ferris; it wasn't easy to get a dollar out of them, but they were great innovators. Danny was a bowling alley owner, a little guy and very shrewd; he and Leo and a scout named Emil Barboni helped to come up with the twenty-four-second clock while I was in Syracuse, and now Danny's in the Hall of Fame.

The whole time I was in Syracuse, I'd go to work with people who were white, and then I'd go home to people who were black, or African American, if you will. Being called "black" doesn't bother me. I'm proud of it, and it's a word I use. *African American* is correct; that's what I am. But I'm proud, very proud, of being black. Coming up, we'd been called niggers, coons, coloreds, but what we were, what joined us, was being black. You know what I'm saying. Being black, and living it, is an integral part of my life. That's why the Fifteenth Ward was so important in Syracuse. Sweets and Chuck Cooper and myself—we had no players' association to smooth things out for us. No one ever did for us what Branch Rickey did for Jackie, because basketball had a little different makeup; whites and blacks had been around each other for a while. There wasn't the same kind of shock when we came in.

Not that we were treated the same. Not even close. For my first few years in the league, there were still some restaurants that would serve you and some that wouldn't—situations like that. Even in Syracuse, there were places I could and couldn't go. But it was always at its worst in the exhibition season, when we'd go into these little tank towns in places like

15. Earl on the 1952–53 Syracuse Nationals. The local newspapers made note of his role as the first African American on the team, but paid little attention to his groundbreaking status in the league. (Courtesy of the Biasone Collection at Le Moyne College)

Missouri. I remember once we arrived by charter bus in Paducah, Kentucky, and as soon as we got there, a taxi was waiting to take the black guys to the other side of the tracks.

It was in Syracuse, really, that I took on the role I'd be remembered for in the NBA, as a guy doing things that people watching the game from the stands won't necessarily appreciate. In college, I'd been a little more of a scorer. Once I got to Syracuse, common sense would tell you that you can't have Dolph Schayes, one of the great scorers in the game, trying to guard the high scorers on the teams we played. We needed his scoring badly, and we wanted him to do what he did best, which means he couldn't get burned out playing defense every night. My job was to complement him.

16. Earl boxing out, during his time in Syracuse. In Syracuse in the 1950s, Earl was asked to put his energy into rebounding and defense. (Courtesy of the Biasone Collection at Le Moyne College)

If he and I played the same kind of game, we wouldn't win. I understood that. So that meant I had to defend their star forwards, sometimes even their centers, to give Dolph a break. My job, night after night, was to guard some of the greatest players of that era.

But if my role had been different? If the chemistry of the team had been different? Yes, I believe I could have scored. I was one of our high scorers in college. In Syracuse, I remember at one point we played Fort Wayne and Philly back-to-back, and I was high scorer both times. But that wasn't often. It wasn't my job. My brother used to say, "You've got to score more, man." I'd tell him, "On that end, I've got to save my energy." I'd go on defense and have one of the league's best scorers bringing it right at me. On offense, the Nats didn't see me as a scorer. My scoring came off hustle points. There were no plays called for me.

We had a simple measuring stick: anytime we held someone under eighty points, we'd win. To hold someone under eighty points, you had to play as a group. There was no way around it. So I knew very quickly what was expected of me: rebounding and defense. You name 'em, I played 'em man-to-man: Neil Johnston. Paul Arizin. Mikan. There's one film clip, and I don't see it that often but I wish I had a copy of it, we were playing a game and I got a defensive rebound and threw it out and ran out to fill the lane and got it back in time to put in the layup on the other end. That was my game. The beauty of it, for me, isn't in the play itself. It's in the hustle, the fundamentals. Today they'd call it a hustle play, and that's one way I hope that I'm remembered. I don't think anyone who ever played against me would deny that I played hard, and it was really the same way with that whole Syracuse team.

The game today is beautiful, and these kids are magnificent, but one thing I don't understand—especially with the ability I see—is how teams can get so many offensive rebounds. Inside the locker room, we had our little slogans. We used to work to keep teams to "eighty or under," and there was one other thing we always said; it was simple math—if you can't control your own backboard, you can't win. But to gain something, you've always got to give up something. And for me, in Syracuse, that something was scoring.

Sure, it could get frustrating. I was being asked to guard George Mikan, which was as hard as anything I'd been asked to do in sports, but I'd do it. No question. You did what you had to do to help the team win. My job, above all else, was defense. When I played a guy, a lot of times he would be bigger than me, and he'd be the best rebounder on the other team. Those guys were going to get face-guarded. That was my only chance. If I looked at the stats the next day, and I saw a guy only had two or three rebounds, that was my twenty points. You understand? I don't know if you get remembered for that, but if you ask, that's how I want to be remembered. I don't call it a sacrifice, because it was my job. If you're up against a high scorer, and you hold him to average or lower, you did a good job. Where teams kill you is if a guy averaging twenty-five goes for forty, and eight of those points come on three or four putbacks. You lose that way, and the coach understands—and the team understands—exactly where you lost, and how it happened.

If you're guarding a guy, even a brilliant guy like Bill Russell, you can't allow him to get to the hoop, because once he's there, the offensive rebound is the easiest shot in the world. I spent a lot of time fighting that battle. You do what you have to do to win. And in the end, you win when the key people, in key moments, get the ball. Our go-to guy, Dolph, was a tremendous go-to guy because he knew what to do with the basketball. He was fearless and had no fear of failing. At the end of the game, you wanted the ball in the hands of a guy like that.

My job, then, was playing defense and helping Dolph save his energy to score. The kids today, I don't know if they recognize the importance of that kind of job. I'll tell you the two toughest guys I ever had to guard:

17. Dolph Schayes, a record-breaking scorer for the Nationals in Syracuse, returns in 1994 to the Blodgett School gymnasium, where the game-changing twenty-four-second shot clock was used for the first time, fifty years earlier. Schayes and Earl were twinned for years at the forward positions for the Nats. (Photo by Dick Blume, courtesy of the *Post-Standard*)

Physically, George Mikan was there. He was tough. He's a guy who's six-ten, who comes out with maybe thirty pounds on you, and he's the biggest star in the league so you can't touch him without a whistle going off. But how about Elgin Baylor? The night before a game, you've always got to go to sleep, but it's not easy going to sleep when you know Elgin's coming.

Now, Elgin's greatness really mattered. It helped bring about more change. You talk about the game the kids play today, the game they love, and I think Elgin is the pioneer. Understand, during his time the league had some legitimate stars, but no one like Elgin. He's getting the ball on the side where he wants it, and he's coming at you and he's got to score, and this is not a guy playing in the style of an Arizin or a Johnston. You want a change in the game, there it is. You've got to dig in.

I remember one time he's at my house for dinner before the game, because that's the way we did it for one another in those times, the way we took care of each other when a guy came to your town. He says to me, "Well, big fella, I'm taking you in deep tonight." And I told him, "Elgin, you come on in, but you're going to pay a terrible price." That was the relationship, the friendship, we all had: try to kill each other on the court, look out for each other off it.

You didn't want those guys just sitting in their hotel rooms. Remember—unless it was New York—at that time in most cities, the black guys still weren't going anyplace. There were still plenty of places in most cities where you weren't wanted. So after the game, no matter how hard-fought it was, if a guy wanted to go someplace and kick back for a beer or some music, it was your job to take him there. And before the game, he might even come to your house and eat. But at game time, man, you'd want to kick the guy's ass.

The players themselves weren't really a problem for us. They knew better than to say too much on the court. But the crowds—that could be a different story. Indianapolis was tough. Fort Wayne was tough. St. Louis was tough. Boston was tough. Baltimore was tough. You heard it. You heard all the words you'd expect. Boston was a big eastern city, and you didn't expect it there at first, but then you got there and you heard it and you knew. You knew fast. In Syracuse, the biggest complaint wasn't the racial stuff. It was the weather. A lot of guys, when they came in, just wanted to stay in the hotel. They all used to complain about the snow, but you didn't see us complaining about it: it was our friend. Anything that upset the Celtics or the Lakers was our friend.

I often get asked about the 1955 team that won the championship, and of course that's a great memory. But the Syracuse team I really remember was from 1954, when we played the Lakers for the championship. Let me tell you, we had six healthy people, and the Lakers were overwhelming favorites, the great dynasty in the game. People thought they were going to kill us. George King had a broken bone, Dolph's wrist was broken, I had a broken bone in my hand, Bill Gabor's knee was all torn up, and we're playing the Lakers, the cream of the crop. We took 'em out to seven games. That was sheer will. Whatever you say about us, we played hard. Al Cervi, our coach, was a tough customer. Al was a funny guy, really. He'd tell you different things, just about anything, to motivate you.

Coaching is a tough job. I remember once, after we'd lost a few games in a row, Al came into the locker room and said, "You aren't going to ruin my family." He said his son came home from school crying because other kids said his daddy was a bum. That's what you call a motivational tool. Al Cervi was a fierce competitor. He wanted to win, and you couldn't help but appreciate that about him. When we went up against that Laker team—Mikkelsen, Mikan, Pollard, guys like that—we played them as hard as we could physically. Size-wise, we were outmanned.

The league at that time was truly a home-and-home thing. Here was Minneapolis, a team that's the premier team in basketball, and what's amazing is that a lot of people could not figure out how we were winning against them. We had one big-name player and a lot of guys who just played really hard and knew what they were doing. The newspaper writers called us "ragtag," but we had people on that team dedicated to one proposition: play hard and win games. The more we were denounced as being small time and small town by other teams around the league, the more it fired us up.

Those were the days of a real home-court advantage, and that advantage had nothing to do with the court. We'd take a train up to Minneapolis from Syracuse, and we'd start with a night train to Chicago. We'd ride all day, your legs pushed up in those seats, and there were times we'd arrive

18. Earl was reunited in 2005 with Ralph Esposito, timekeeper for the old Syracuse Nationals, during the unveiling of a Syracuse monument to the twenty-four-second shot clock. (Photo by Dennis Nett, courtesy of the *Post-Standard*)

at three, three thirty in the afternoon. You'd barely have time to eat and take a nap, and it would be game time. You more or less had been up all night, and your tank was really low, and we were already hurt, and we were playing against maybe the greatest team in the history of the game to that point.

We played Minneapolis in those conditions. That was still a year before the twenty-four-second clock came in, and they could afford to wait on Mikan when they played. He'd get the rebound and toss it out, and they'd take their time waiting for him to get upcourt. He wasn't fleet of foot. Before the clock, he didn't need to be. Not so strange, a year later, once the clock came in, that we won it.

We were banged up, but the only way to beat the Lakers was to run. You had to make them pay on the other end. I had to guard Mikan, and whenever we were in transition, I'd run hard and someone else would have to pick me up, and that would free one of our quicker guys and we tried to take advantage of the situation. You hoped the man grabbing you was Dolph's man, so Dolph would be free. Those seem like little things, but we had guys who were smart, and that was our only chance. We watched and saw how their big guys ran right down the middle of the floor. We knew: Stay away from the middle. Go to the side. We'd try to hit those little jumpers from the baseline or outside.

Mikan was a big, strong guy, and what a lot of people don't remember is that when he was playing, it was a six-foot lane. That big man and a six-foot lane. How could you stop him? Now it's a little different. These guys we played against would have had a little trouble with the bigger lane today. They couldn't possibly be as effective. But in those days, with those conditions, with those rules, once George got down there and set up, you had a problem. I'd try to "front" him, but it was hard to get around him once he spread out; to get around him you had to cut a wide swath. In the end, you just tried to take away the real easy shots. You tried to make him earn every point, without easy putbacks.

Then we had Vern Mikkelsen to deal with, who was as big as Mikan, nearly. Both teams played hard—they gave no quarter—but I don't remember any physical confrontations. You just got so tired and physically drained that all you could think about was playing the game. There was so much emotion, and we couldn't afford to spend it by shooting off our mouths. We were shorthanded, but we never used it as an excuse. Looking back, it is utterly amazing that we took them to seven games before we lost.

I really believe what we did in the 1953–54 playoffs, for us, was as monumental as winning it all. To go that far, under those conditions . . . You can go through the annals of the NBA, and it's still something special. I'd broken my hand in New York. I was going up for a rebound, and a Knick guy came up behind me and his elbow hit the back of my hand, and it just snapped. The next day I was in a hospital in Syracuse getting a cast put on it, and then I was ready to play. That was it. It was my shooting hand, and I knew if I was going to do any scoring, it would be layups.

The series ended in Minnesota; we lost the seventh game. After it was over, I was as tired as I'd ever been in my life. What I didn't know is that we were going to get a new center, a kid named John Kerr, who would be our missing piece. And I couldn't know the twenty-four-second clock was going to change everything, and that we'd just seen the end of the Laker dynasty.

9

The Ice Bucket

I spent most of my NBA years in Syracuse. I didn't have many problems there, but a couple of things happened that stay with me today. Syracuse wasn't the worst place, and it wasn't the best place: it was the way most northern cities were at the time. That meant they didn't put up signs that said "Colored only," but you still found out real fast where you could and couldn't go.

During my years in Syracuse I stayed with the Sylvahns, on East Fayette Street. They were a special couple. They ran a newspaper for the black community, because the big papers there pretty much ignored us, the same way it had been in West Virginia. If you got arrested, you might be in the paper, but that was about it. Along with the paper, the Sylvhans also ran a boardinghouse. It didn't take me long to realize I needed to find a place to live in the Fifteenth Ward, because I wasn't leaving that neighborhood. The Sylvahns were a nice couple; they took me in like one of their own. She was white and he was black, which was very unusual at that time. It was also sad because of the usual craziness. Her sisters would come to see her, but they wouldn't come into the house; she would have to go outside and sit in the car with them.

Mrs. Sylvahn treated me like the son she never had, and sometimes I would get out and around the neighborhood with a couple of good friends: Eugene Williams and Don Caldwell, although I called them "Moon" and "Peewee." That's how it was in those days. The players today can stay wherever they want. But I had to live in this little area where all the blacks stayed in Syracuse, and that did a lot to keep you humble. You were reminded all the time that what you did just didn't make all that much difference, not with the things that really mattered.

For me, it was time for more handprints: Moon and Peewee made that city feel like home.

Moon is gone now, but Peewee, a retired post office clerk, is still there. The last time I was in Syracuse they had an event for the old Nats, and someone said to me, "Didn't you just love our city?" And I said, "You see those two men? That's what I loved about Syracuse." Because we would sit on the porch and try to solve the troubles of the world, and my world was what they called the Fifteenth Ward. Every black person I knew in Syracuse lived there, and they took care of me: nothing bad was ever going to happen to me in the Fifteenth Ward. At first, maybe those folk expected I'd be different or have some airs because of basketball, but I think they eventually came to see me as just a decent human being.

I lived on Fayette Street, and my social life outside the team pretty much consisted of walking to the Embassy (jazz club), which I'll really get into later in the book. They had a real jazzy jukebox and they had some great live performers, and they always kept orange soda in the cooler for me, because I never drank alcohol. I'd go to the Embassy and play three or four tunes on the box to get ready to play, and then I'd go to the game. I remember once someone told Danny Biasone, our owner, they'd seen me in there drunk. Danny knew the truth. Sure. Earl was drunk on that orange soda.

In those days, there was no real escape from the realities of race. There was no refuge, like there'd been at West Virginia State. It was everywhere, with some towns worse than others. Bobby Hopkins was with me in Syracuse, this guy who came up to play with us from Grambling, where he'd led the nation in scoring. I submit to you that he had all the tools. Once he learned the nuances of the game on the NBA level, it would have been "Watch out." But he hurt his knee one summer, and that was it for his career. If he had stayed healthy, what a player he would have been. While he was there, he was like a younger brother to me, and I figured he'd be the guy who'd take my place someday in the lineup. And of course, since he was black, he and I were often together in experiencing the way things were.

19. Earl *(third from left)* and his Syracuse Nationals teammates rejoice with owner Danny Biasone after defeating the Philadelphia Warriors in the NBA Eastern Division playoffs in 1957. Paul Seymour is shaking Biasone's hand; Al Bianchi is sitting on the ground. *Standing, from left:* trainer Art Van Auken, who taught Earl to drive; Joe Holup; Earl; Johnny Kerr; Bob Harrison; Bobby Hopkins; Dolph Schayes; Togo Palazzi; and Ed Conlin. In the entire seventeen-year existence of the Syracuse franchise, the team never missed the playoffs. (Courtesy of the *Post-Standard*)

This is what I mean when I say some towns were worse than others: Bobby and I were in St. Louis one time, and we got out and walked around and didn't even see black guys working construction, and we walked past a barbershop and a white kid was shining shoes. Think of that. In that town, they wouldn't even let a black kid shine shoes! And we looked at each other, and we knew what to expect. Didn't have to say a word. Sure enough, when we ran onto the court, the first thing we heard was, "Look at that. They got niggers on the team." We didn't react. I believed then what I believe now: never, ever dignify ignorance.

So I guess compared to that, Syracuse wasn't so bad. It was the right place at the right time, because there were much worse places. Based on that, I'll give Syracuse a pass. I got there in 1952, and Syracuse was like any town for black folks, even in Upstate New York. They had restricted covenants on the homes that made sure certain people lived in certain neighborhoods. The one part of town with black people was the Fifteenth Ward, even if you played professional basketball. That's the way it was, and you lived it. You had to follow it. You couldn't even laugh about it at the time, but things would change. They always change.

As far as the team goes in Syracuse, I only had a couple of problems. One year, when I was the only black on the team, they scheduled an exhibition in Greenville, South Carolina. They came to me and said, "We're leaving you home." The deal was, no black dudes could play or they would call off the game, and the Nats ownership wanted the game. Management chose to schedule the game knowing I would not be allowed to participate. That's how management did it in those days. The problem I had was with my teammates. I needed one thing, and one thing only. Someone should have come to me and said, "Listen, they scheduled that game for us, and you can't play and that's not right." But no one did. No one came to me. Not one person.

That's a test, and it didn't exactly leave a scar, but you look at people differently after that. We had always been considered a closely knit team. Once that game was scheduled, my teammates had to play. There was no players' association to protect us. But if the situation was reversed, I'd like to think I'd approach my teammates and say, "This game was scheduled by management. We've got to play, but it's not right."

The South Carolina situation made me quietly assess and reassess my own importance, as a player and as a human being. I had another teammate, I remember we went to a party at his house, and he had a statue of a black jockey on his lawn. I told the guy, "That offends me." He explained to me how there was nothing wrong with it, and I said to him, "As long as you have that out there, I'd prefer you didn't invite me." I asked him if he would ever put a statue out there of a drunken Irishman hanging from a light pole. He couldn't understand, and I couldn't understand why he couldn't understand why I was upset. I said to him, "You read. You watch television. You ever just stop and ask yourself why there are no black folks in your neighborhood? You think we all live where we live by choice alone?" He had no answer for that, but the statue didn't come down.

There would be other times in my career when people stood up: Bones McKinney in Washington. Freddy Scolari, who spoke up for me when the Capitols broke up. Dick McGuire in Detroit. You remember those things forever. That's all I needed in Syracuse, for just one person to say, "Earl, this isn't right." But no one did. And you realize in the end that you're alone.

Once in a while, something would happen that gave you hope. George King, who was with the Nats when I got there, played his college ball at a little school in West Virginia. He played at Morris Harvey in Charleston, and I played a few miles away at West Virginia State, but our schools would never have played against each other, because his team was all white, mine all black. I knew of him because the newspapers in Charleston that never would write about us were full of stories about George and his exploits. So one day in Syracuse, a player on another team was giving him a hard time, working him over, stuff that we considered going too far. So I said to George, "Bring him my way."

It wasn't something I would just have done for George. It would have been for anybody. You can't just let other teams pound on your people. If you're going to do that to one of our guys, you're going to pay a price. So George brought him to me, and I set the pick the certain way I had to set it, and the guy learned the lesson. He learned real quick. There was no fighting, because he understood. He knew what he had been doing, and he knew what I was doing, and he knew my job was to protect my teammate. After that, he played George with a little more respect. This is what I'm saying, the difference between what I could do and Jackie couldn't, why I have so much respect for him: I had recourse, quiet recourse. In baseball, you're alone down on that field.

George King and I would become good friends. He was my man, and once you got to know his wife, you understood why he was the man he was. They were just fine people. So you had these two guys from West Virginia, from completely different worlds, and they became good friends.

Those are the ways I hang on to hope. Our trainer, Art Van Auken, made life easier for me in Syracuse. Early on, I was without a vehicle. Every day, for practice, Art would pick me up at my boardinghouse and then give me a ride home. He drove an Oldsmobile, and he took the time to take me to a cemetery in Syracuse for a private driving lesson. I got my driver's license and my first car in Syracuse, and I owe part of that to Art.

People now, I know they say I was an enforcer. I didn't look at it that way. But I was encouraged to do what Jackie couldn't. They beat him down and said, "Turn the other cheek," and no one ever told me anything like that. In basketball, to say that to one of your big guys, that would be competitive suicide. If someone's bothering you and you don't take care of it, you give up easy baskets and your team will lose. A coach who let that go would be stupid. Now if a guy on the other team is punishing one of our smaller players, I'd say, "Bring him to me, and bring him real hard." The guy is concentrating on his man, and you firm up your body, make it real taut, and you get ready and the ref is looking the other way, and then "Boom!," and maybe you add a little icing to it. You set a pick, and whatever juice you can add to it, you do it. I had that recourse. Jackie didn't.

I can truthfully say that I was never called a racial name by a player. That came sometimes from the stands, but never from the players. I'd only get upset if somebody hit me too hard or caught me when I wasn't looking, and that could happen to everyone on the court. We played against teams that would be real brave when we were on the road, but their attitudes were much different in Syracuse. There was a reason we had a great home record. The weather was brutal, and our fans, they were really loyal. Crazy, even. I remember we lost once by twenty, and the fans were out there after the game screaming that it was the refs' fault. It wasn't Sid Borgia taking away our easy rebounds, but our fans had unbelievable faith in us. What our fans got away with then, I don't know if they could get away with now. But I'm not surprised that Syracuse still puts those big crowds in the house at the Carrier Dome. Those people love their basketball.

The only other problem I remember with a teammate was in one of my first practices when I got to Syracuse. This guy was tough—that was his whole reputation—and we're practicing at the Y in Syracuse. I set a pick, and he came into me and threw an elbow, a very dangerous elbow that could have really done some damage. Practice continued, and when it was done I pulled him aside and said, "Look, there's a good chance we'll be teammates and I don't want to get off on the wrong foot. But if you don't change what you're doing, one of us is going to get hurt. Given a choice, it's not going to be me." That did it. We were never bosom buddies, but we came to a quick understanding. He was a good teammate, and we took care of each other on the court.

The year after the Lakers beat us was our big year, the year when we finally won it all, and two things made the difference: We had Johnny Kerr, a real center, and the game had really changed. Danny and Leo Ferris had pushed through the twenty-four-second clock, and Mikan had retired, and it was the right moment in history for a team of hard workers who loved to run the court. We got to the finals against the Fort Wayne Pistons, and we knew it was going to be tough, but I think we got a little advantage when they had to move their home games to Indianapolis because they had something going on in their own arena.

I knew I'd hear just about everything from fans in Indianapolis. That was a place where you heard the worst stuff, but they were rough on all of us: I remember someone throwing a chair once and almost hitting George King. All of that added to a tremendous rivalry with Fort Wayne. It was a tough, physical championship series, and they had us down when we came home for the last two games. We won the first one, and then played for the championship on Easter Sunday. We were down three games to two when we came home, and Fort Wayne let it slip away. I know a lot of their players always insisted they were the better team and they got robbed. What history records is the team that won four games, and the champion of the league that year was Syracuse.

In the last game, we fell behind in the first half by sixteen or seventeen, and we knew we had to stay within striking distance. A year earlier, without the clock, Fort Wayne would have held the ball, and we would have been in big trouble, but with the shot clock they couldn't stall. We were a very persistent team, and we kept pecking away and pecking away, and you look up and all of a sudden you're tied and there's not much time left.

That's when big-time players make big-time plays, and George King made the biggest play of his career. He got fouled and went to the line. George was a terrible free-throw shooter, and I'm sure Fort Wayne assumed he would miss the shot. When he went to the line I said, "Lord have mercy. Anybody but George." But he stepped up like he knew what he was doing and made the shot. Then he stole the ball, and that was it. We were world champions.

I was the first black guy to start on a championship team, which is hard to process when you take a look at the great players and the great

20. The NBA champions of 1955. *Front row, left to right:* Paul Seymour, Billy Kenville, Wally Osterkorn, Dick Farley, George King, and Coach Al Cervi. *Back row:* Red Rocha, Jim Tucker, John Kerr, Earl, and Dolph Schayes. (Courtesy of the Biasone Collection at Le Moyne College)

teams that have come along since then. I don't remember anyone saying much about it. We had a party afterward, I think at Danny's bowling alley, but it wasn't like it is today. We didn't even get rings. They gave us an ice bucket. Basketball didn't have that kind of notoriety. The best players in the world played for teams in Milwaukee and Syracuse and Rochester and Fort Wayne, which many people didn't see as exactly major league.

But it was major league. It was the best of basketball. And my team was the champion of the world.

10

Jazz

Here's one subject that is worth a chapter by itself. It involves one of the great passions in my life. In Syracuse, where I could have felt alone, it's the medium that drew me and Donald "Peewee" Caldwell and Eugene "Moon" Williams together: jazz.

Throughout your life, you hear music and you gravitate to the kind that moves you. A lot of my friends in high school were listening to groups like the Ink Spots. Me and a couple of other classmates, we were Billy Eckstine fans, and that got us started. I just fell in love with jazz. When I was playing in the NBA in the 1950s, I brought my *Down Beat* magazine on every trip I took. There was a section in *Down Beat* that told you where the top jazz clubs could be found in most of the major cities. After every game, I'd find my way to one of those clubs.

The premier city for music was New York, and the premier jazz club was definitely Birdland. Baltimore and Washington had good jazz, and so did Philadelphia. Even Minneapolis had a couple of really fine clubs. I listened to just about all these guys at one place or another, and the one I got to know best was Les McCann, just a really fine piano player.

There had been nothing like that available when we were kids. There was nothing available to us, period. There was quite a bit of time when there was no electricity in my home, so there was no radio. It's hard to sit where I'm sitting today and imagine that. You used kerosene lamps around the house, which wasn't real healthy, but you did what you had to do. Later on, when we got the place in the projects, we had electricity and we could sit around with the radio, and there was no real competition for it: my mother spent her time singing hymns around the house. As long as

I stayed out of trouble, my mother and father weren't worried about me listening to the music that I loved.

I was a junior in college when I first heard great jazz, and it changed me, just listening to guys like Miles Davis and Dexter Gordon. In 1950 a guy named Jimmy Smith jumped onto the scene who was a tremendous jazz organist, and pretty soon most nightclubs had jazz organ trios. I've been a jazz organ fan ever since. Now I can find a jazz channel on cable, and cool jazz on the radio, but if I really want to hear something I love, I dig into my stack of CDs looking for the guys from that era.

When Dexter Gordon died, I told my wife, "We've got to have a memorial," and I played his stuff for a month. Finally Charlita said, "Earl, the memorial was fine. Now it's time for a Christian burial."

I remember there was a guy named Ed Mosler in New York, a real booster of the Nats, who was associated with a company that made safes. After we'd get done playing the Knicks he'd always want to take us out. There was a group called the Three Suns, and they played accordion, and one night he had tickets. Now, to each his own. This guy wanted to go, and he had great seats, but we were in New York, home of Birdland, the most celebrated jazz club in the world. I said to him, "There's no way I can waste your money sitting there, pretending to like your music, when Dexter Gordon and Miles Davis are holding forth."

We all need things in our lives we're passionate about. I was passionate about basketball, but when the game was over, you need a way to exhale. For me, jazz was relaxation.

Funny thing is, I'd be in the clubs all that time, but I didn't drink. I never learned how. In college, on one or two occasions, I tried a beer. I just never learned to like it. I never made a big deal of it, or ran around telling people I didn't drink, but it's just something I felt no need to do. Even today, when we have parties or any social situation at our house, we don't serve booze, and everyone seems to enjoy themselves. I never saw drinking as a prerequisite for having fun.

I will make this point: today, people say, "Earl, you look pretty good," and I don't think any of this is coincidence. There are things that ravage your body, things I saw ravage a lot of bodies, that I never did. Even hanging out real late was never a big option for me. I've always been a proponent of rest. Even when I'm with people I love, I know when to go to bed. In Syracuse, at midnight, I was home or on my way.

It went back a long way for me. When I was a kid, when people were drinking, they weren't drinking mixed drinks. They were hitting the scotch and water or bourbon and water. Some of them were real two-fisted drinkers, and I recall watching them drink and how they contorted their faces as it went down. I'd ask the question, "Why would you do that to yourself?"

My role models were my parents. My mother never smoked or drank. My father tasted it a little bit, but basically I was around quiet people. Then I became an athlete, and that's a very controlled atmosphere. If my high school coach, Coach Johnson, found out you were smoking or drinking, that was it. You were gone. And I wasn't going to disappoint him—or my parents—in that way.

The whole environment worked against it. Anyone who was a friend of my parents felt free to discipline me, and all of them wanted me to succeed. Try to discipline some of these kids today, and you'll get yourself killed. Things are upside down. In my town, school was the social event of the day, and you wanted to be there. But if you skipped it and an older person saw you in the street, they'd tell your parents, and they'd tell you they were going to call your parents. And you said nothing, because the last thing you wanted to hear from your mother was, "You sassed her?" No, no, no! It was totally unacceptable. I had plenty of respect for my mother, but I didn't fear her discipline. I feared her disappointment.

That was my upbringing. The kids today might laugh at it, but it's what gave me a chance. You look at the way things are going today, with these kids on the street when they're still in grade school, completely out of control, and you wonder how we're ever going to get back to the way it was for us when we were kids. But we have to do it. We have to find a way. Disrespect for others, disrespect for yourself, that's what destroys you.

I wonder what kind of a difference it would make if these kids were raised with the knowledge they were loved by all the adults around them, and if we taught these children as soon as they could walk about the sac-rifices made for them by all the folks who came before, and then I wonder if we'd even need to worry about discipline. Because they'd know. They'd know what was expected of them. That will guide you and direct you, even when you've been around as long as I have.

There was very little temptation available to us. If we did go some-place that we shouldn't be, adults would tell us to get out of there. We were green. These kids today, they've seen and heard everything. We were in a small town, and I played three sports in high school, and that kept me busy. And my parents explained all the crazy stuff that could happen to us, and where we ought to be and where we shouldn't be.

In Alexandria, there was always a hand that was going to touch your life: your parents, your parents' friends, your teachers. You had to have genuine respect for your elders. If you got on the bus and an elderly female got on the bus, you had better stand up and let her have that seat. That's how it was. That same attitude existed, even more so, when we traveled to different cities. My parents would tell me, "People will judge us by how you conduct yourself. Conduct yourself accordingly," and accordingly is what they raised me to do.

My parents never had it easy. To be black in Alexandria in the 1920s and '30s and '40s meant that you were treated like you were subhuman. If white folks were first class, we didn't qualify as second. Fourth class is more like it. And I grew up watching my parents being treated that way.

Believe me, if you saw a police officer, you didn't think he was there to help. You got out of there, before he found something to arrest you for. Whatever it was, if you got to court, they'd find you guilty. That was America, and that's why it was such a joke to me, all these people upset about the Reverend Wright saying angry things. Of course people are still angry. If you want to, you can pretend they're not, but that doesn't change how people feel after they've spent most of their lives being forced to question their own worth as human beings. It's going to take a lot of years, and a lot of work, to change those feelings.

That's why I say I'm far more worried about the way you remember me as a person, as a guy trying to live up to what his parents expected, than as a ballplayer. Being a ballplayer was fine, a wonderful thing for me, and it opened a lot of doors. But the basketball court is only where everything that I'd been taught played out.

Those were still hard times, and you still walked off the court into reality. So when I was beaten down, or sick of it, I'd go and find some jazz.

11

Exclamation

I've always talked about handprints. Whatever we accomplish, it's because someone else puts their hands on us positively. It's been true for me at every important moment in my life. It was true on the day I became a coach.

I'd been traded from Syracuse to Detroit in 1958. Enter Dick McGuire. He was a guard, and I played with him on the Pistons for a year. Then I played for him for a year, in the 1959–60 season, when Fred Zollner hired him as the coach. Dick didn't talk a whole lot, but when he talked, it was like E. F. Hutton: you needed to listen. Before the 1960 season, out of the clear blue, he offered me an assistant coach's job. I say that like it was matter-of-fact, but you've got to stop and think of what that meant. We weren't a whole lot past a time when they didn't trust a black player enough to let him run an offense. With Dick, there was no hand-wringing, nothing gut-wrenching. He didn't treat it like it was a monumental decision. I'm not saying there weren't other people around who wanted to make decisions like that, but that's the difference at any time, the quality that sets some people above the rest. Dick didn't worry about it. He just did it.

Now, you remember how I told you I owed a debt to Wilt Chamberlain. I was thirty-two, and I wasn't sure I was ready to quit. Dick had made it very clear that the job was mine if I wanted it. I said, "Let me go through training camp, through the exhibition season, and then we can decide." We went to Hershey, Pennsylvania, for an exhibition game against the Philadelphia Warriors. Wilt was on the floor. He was seven-foot-something. After seeing him for the first time, that was the clincher. The decision was a no-brainer. I went to Dick and said, "I'll take that job."

In my acceptance speech at the Naismith Memorial Basketball Hall of Fame, I went through the whole thing, all the great people who'd put their hands on me in life, from my parents to that elementary school teacher named Helen Day to the people who cared about me in high school and college. I talked about Bill Sharman, such a fantastic guy, and Fred Zollner in Detroit and Dave Bing and Danny Biasone and Bob Lanier and Freddy Scolari, who got me my chance in Syracuse. There were about fourteen people in the Hall of Fame who left handprints all over me. I went through these people alphabetically. They were each important in their own way. But I saved Dick for last, because he made a monumental decision based only on one guy respecting another guy, and thinking his choice was the right one for the job.

Keep in mind that the first black player had been signed into the league only ten years earlier. Now I'm an assistant coach, and I remember a game in San Francisco—about two years after I was hired—and the team's on the floor and I'm watching in a suit and tie. I always wanted to look the part, because I'd spent my whole life learning what can happen if a black man shows up in the wrong attire. Plenty of places, they'd ask you to leave, and this was one job I didn't want to be asked to leave. The Warriors left Philadelphia and moved to San Francisco in 1962, so this had to be one of our first trips out there.

A guy in the stands looks at me and says, "What's the matter? Are you injured?'" It's unfortunate, but those were the times. In a way, I understood. I had no predecessor. He couldn't imagine. There had never been a black assistant coach on the bench. I didn't really answer him, but I'd love to know what he thought when he realized I was an assistant coach.

Dick gave me a free hand. My title was "assistant coach and head scout." Don't be overly impressed with the title. Not only was I the head scout, I was the only scout. On the bench, as an assistant, I was never a black coach. I was a coach who happened to be black. But I was definitely a player's coach.

I was an assistant coach for eight years. I retired to take a job with the Dodge division of the Chrysler Corporation, but Butch Van Breda Kolff quit as Detroit's coach ten games into the 1971 season. The Pistons called and offered me the job, and I signed a two-year contract. It was an easy decision. I had a sense of obligation. These people had been very good to me at Detroit, and now they needed some help. It wasn't the most opportune time. I had a career going with a major corporation. But I had ascended through all the other steps—player, scout, assistant coach. And I was only the second African American, after Bill Russell, to get that chance. You had to take it.

The owner, Fred Zollner, was the guy who hired me. He was a dynamic guy. Here he is, not long after being in Fort Wayne, one of the toughest places I ever had to play, a place where you heard all the choice words, and he hired me as head coach. When he asked me who I wanted as an assistant, I said to him, "Ray Scott is my man. I've got a list of one." Ray was a guy I trusted, and I knew how well he knew the game. Zollner went for it, and I told Ray, "The job is yours." That put him into a good position. When they fired me, he became head coach, and by his second year he was "Coach of the Year."

Zollner could have said no to me about Ray, and he never would have been criticized. That was one of the first all-black coaching combinations in the league, and plenty of people would have thought one black coach was enough—but Zollner didn't. He asked what I wanted, and he gave it to me. If you're a coach, that's what you need from the owner.

Being the head coach was my last job in basketball. I took over in mid-season, and we didn't fare well. We were losing, and then we started the next season the same way and we were going down fast, and they made a change. I accepted that. The day you sign a contract to coach, you're also signing your termination papers. I knew that. The owners just reserve the right to pick the date.

Ray took over and did a great job, but a firing is never amiable. You take it like it comes. I can look back now and say some things just aren't in the cards, and a long NBA coaching career was not in the cards for me. At the time, you have a lot of regrets. You feel as if they're saying to you, "You're not good enough to do this," and we'd all had enough of that in our lives. But like Russ said, you go to war with what they give you.

I'll tell you how it was: The guy I worked for gave me every chance to succeed. The days of the first black players in the league weren't all that far in the past, and I never considered myself a black coach. I just considered myself a coach who happened to be black.

During all those years, I lived in Detroit. Even then, a lot of neighborhoods had restrictive covenants, so we were Detroiters, right in the city. And if you're a Detroiter, you're loyal to Detroit, which is why the team now can never be the Detroit Pistons to me. They play in Auburn Hills. They're not of or from Detroit.

It's important for me to say what Detroit meant to me. For my family, it was a kind of big black butterfly thing. It was the home of Dave Bing, whose handprints are still on my life. It was the place where I met Charlita, my wife and my best friend. Once I got to Detroit, there were a lot of people around who simply weren't going to let me get hurt. I ended up living there for forty-two years, longer than I lived in any one place in my life. That's why I always called it home.

When I arrived in Detroit in 1958, it was more viable than it is today. There were still a lot of black home owners. Sure, there were a few businesses boarded up, but it still felt healthy. It's kind of sad what's going on there now. The real problems started in the early 1970s with the oil embargo, because whenever there are problems with oil, there are big problems in Detroit. It was like a domino effect. First the big auto industry gets hurt, and there are layoffs, and that ripples into all the little places making parts, the places people don't even think about. And now the auto industry is in terrible trouble.

I was there for the riots in 1967. I saw them firsthand. When people have been oppressed and suppressed for years, that's dangerous. It's like gasoline, just waiting for a match. That's what happened. The staging area for the National Guard was this large school complex, and it would be strange: you're on the main drag of this American city, driving home, and here comes a tank. They'd tell you to stay off the streets after dark, and I'm a commonsense person. That's what I did.

But one day I'm standing in line at a bank or at a store, and this white guy is talking, and he's wondering why black folks are burning down their own neighborhoods. I said, "Listen. If you had rats biting your kids' toes at night, you might want to burn the place down, too. Maybe if they had burned them down sooner, their kids would have a decent place to live." He didn't say much. There wasn't much to say. There's always going to be rebellion waiting to happen if people are forced to

21. Earl and Charlita, in Las Vegas in 2006, enjoying a retirement in which they never sit still for long. (Photo by Joe Crowell Jr., courtesy of Earl and Charlita Lloyd)

live in ghettos with no hope of getting out. Unless you've lived it, you probably really shouldn't talk about it, unless you think maybe, in some way, you can help.

During the day it would be kind of quiet, but once the last ray of light was gone, all hell would break loose. When it gets dark, a whole lot of cowards get real brave, which is the story of the riots, and the story of the Klan, and a story really that's as old as man.

After coaching, I went to work for the Dodge division of the Chrysler Corporation. They said to me, "We've got twenty-six regional offices, and we don't have a single black person in any of them, because we can't find anyone who's qualified." That was my job, to recruit minorities, and I said to my director, a great guy, "If you're sure you want to hire qualified black people, I'll find them. But just be sure."

Before long, he was saying, "Where do you keep finding these people?" I could understand why he didn't know. If you live your life in blinders, and you never really see into this other world, how could you know about the huge cadre of qualified people out there who just want to work? There were guys with college degrees working in post offices, because no one would hire them. It was my job to find those people.

Then I went to the best job I ever had outside of a basketball court: I was a civilian deputy chief in the Detroit Police Department. I was director of the PAL program, the Police Athletic League, and my job description was to work with youth. Every breath you take, you're helping kids move ahead in life. When you do that, you look forward to going to work.

From there I went into the Detroit schools, and I taught young kids employability skills, and that helped them to go out and get jobs. It was the same thing I'd known all along: there are always plenty of folks who want to work, and plenty of kids who want to do it right in life. It wasn't so different from when I was young: if they knew an adult believed in them, and cared about them, it made all the difference.

I finally retired in 1993, and my wife retired as a teacher in 1997, and I thought that was it. I was done. But then Dave Bing called me and said he needed help. He ran a successful steel plant, and he was going from two companies to five. Everyone in Detroit thought they could pick up the phone and just call him, and he was getting tired of having to take all those calls, and I became his director of community relations.

That's one of my favorite stories, the way we met. Dave came out of college in the same year as Cazzie Russell, a big star who went to Michigan, and everyone in the state wanted us to get Cazzie. So the Knicks and the Pistons had a coin flip for the first choice, and we lost. The whole community felt like dying, except for me. I told our people, "Don't worry." I'd scouted Dave at Syracuse, a school that was just starting to achieve, and I knew Detroit would be pleasantly surprised at what it got. Dave was a great player. If you asked the Lord to pick a guy for your team, this is the kind of guy he'd send you: fantastic ability, a role model, not a single derogatory thing about the guy, on or off the court.

Years later, I ended up going to work for him, another job I loved. The job allowed me to be around young kids a lot, and I got to counsel them. I'd tell them, "Any job that pays a decent wage and you're not stealing, be

22. Earl outside his home in Fairfield Glade, Tennessee, in 2000, where he and Charlita have spent their retirement years: a long journey from a childhood in Jim Crow America. (Courtesy of the *Post-Standard*)

proud of that." I could have done it forever, but Charlita retired, and we decided we would finally stop working and go to Tennessee.

Then the schools passed a bond issue to get some buildings repaired. They asked Dave if he could loan them someone to make sure the work was properly done, and he said, "The only person I trust for this is Earl." I put off retirement and did the job, because Dave means that much to me, although Charlita had to spend some time down South in our new home by herself. Finally, I got down there, and we had our chance to retire. And that's where we watched Obama get elected.

Epilogue

Lloyd on Obama, Part Two

A telephone conversation with Earl on November 4, 2008, the night Barack Obama was elected president.

My wife is here crying. We're both crying. You know what this means? I've got grandchildren. For the first time in my life, I can look these kids in the face and tell them they can aspire to be anything they want to be when they grow up. Anything. That's just amazing.

Our president-elect will not be a miracle worker, and he knows he'll have to surround himself with bright people. We wanted the smartest person around to win the election. He's smart enough and cool enough. He knows what he is and who he is, and that's the key.

You know what impressed me? In his speech tonight, he said that he knew fifty-nine million people didn't vote for him. He made a comment that he would also be their president. Those were the folks I think he really wanted to address. His acceptance speech tells me that he's going to be a great president.

In my lifetime, I've now witnessed two miracles. If anybody had tried to convince me that the first black governor in these United States would be the governor of Virginia, I'd have asked them, "What have you been smoking?" Doug Wilder was the first miracle. The second, in my wildest imagination, you could have never convinced me that this country would have a president who happens to be black.

Charlita and I were watching when they finally made it official, and if you want the one word to describe what we felt, it was *pride*. Pride beyond words. The news crews had gone to Spelman College in Atlanta, and there was one student on her knees, sobbing, her face in her hands. If you know your history, there's no way that moment doesn't bring some tears. Given my life, the trials and tribulations I've seen, there's no way you don't cry a river. Just to see him and his beautiful family, and to know they're going to be living in the White House: it's just an electrical moment you know you'll never stop savoring.

Tonight's speech was the best I've heard during the whole election. He wasn't ranting or raving. He showed a calm hand. He's got the support of this whole universe, and he's got political capital, and he's smart enough to use it properly. People are hurting monetarily, and he understands: that's where he can bring us together. You know that's what he's working on right now. He'll have a steady hand at the helm. I'll say it again: this man was anointed. You tell me what black politician we have going right now who could have survived Reverend Wright—twice! He survived because he never got angry, he never got defensive, he never tried to hoodwink anybody. Most people go to churches where you disagree sometimes with what your preacher says, but you don't jump up and run out. He didn't get defensive. He didn't get angry. He just let it rise and fall.

I looked at Jesse Jackson crying in the audience, and people had the audacity to question if it was for real. Trust me. Those tears were very real. Think of the experience Jesse Jackson had. He was there on the night Dr. King was killed. Coming from all of that, how could he not cry? Look, I've had a lot of honors bestowed upon me, a lot of fantastic blessings bestowed upon me. But I would wrap them up in a box and put a pretty bow on it with a smiley face and hand it to you in return for what I'm feeling right now. You could have it all, just for this one moment.

I stood on somebody's shoulders and somebody stood on mine and somebody stood on theirs, and President Obama is the ultimate recipient of millions and millions of people doing that. Handprints! The handprints are everywhere! You cannot go by yourself from being a black baby born in 1928 in Virginia and here you are, a member of the basketball Hall of Fame, watching on the night the president-elect happens to be a black man. You cannot negotiate that journey by yourself. No way. You were a black baby whose life was a question mark, a black baby who so easily could be lost to the history books, but your life became an exclamation mark.

And then you see this, what happened tonight.

(Earl paused to compose himself.)

I think Obama understands all this. Watching the way he treats his family, the way he speaks about his grandparents, he definitely understands. For me, at every major stop along the way, there was nothing for me but a whole lot of love. My youngest son, David, got married a few months ago, and I said to him, "I know you're madly in love, and I'm sure you intend to stay in love. But when you truly love someone, nothing's impossible, not for you, not for them." I've got four grandchildren, and I don't have to sugarcoat things anymore. When I tell them things have changed, I can point at the White House.

I'm sitting here thinking about my teachers, a teacher like Helen Day, who would have given us anything she had. I'm thinking about my parents, about my mother, and what a fighter she was. Without those people, we were destined to lose, to disappear one by one. That's why my heart breaks when I think about the kids today, why in some ways they've got it even harder than us: I think sometimes they have no one like that in their corner, and you've got to have someone. Or you've got to find your way to someone.

That's what I was trying to explain to David: you've got to find the love that can take you anywhere.

Appendix A | Appendix B | Index

Appendix A

Sean Kirst on Earl Lloyd
and the Fifteenth Ward

Over the years, as a columnist with the *Post-Standard* in Syracuse, I've had the good fortune to chronicle some important moments in the life of Earl Lloyd. I spoke with him shortly after his enshrinement into the Naismith Memorial Basketball Hall of Fame. I joined him for an emotional return to his old campus at West Virginia State University. Occasionally, in situations that had absolutely nothing to do with basketball—such as a time when community leaders were debating a residency rule for city teachers—Earl provided me with telling insight.

We include a handful of those columns and articles in this appendix, reprinted with the permission of the *Post-Standard*. They speak not only to Earl's experience but to the memorable Fifteenth Ward community that surrounded him in Syracuse in the 1950s—including a few extraordinary men and women mentioned in the book, such as the Sylvahns and "Lottie the Body" Graves. All told, they are part of the texture of Earl's triumph.

"Lloyd, Biasone Forever Changed the Game"
September 22, 2000

Manny Breland was a quiet listener Wednesday in a room at Le Moyne College. He stood in the back as the Danny Biasone Tribute Committee announced a daylong celebration surrounding the founder of the old Syracuse Nationals, a Syracuse guy just elected to the Basketball Hall of Fame. As part of the Nov. 29 festivities, the committee also plans to honor Earl Lloyd, who spent his best years in basketball playing for Biasone.

The mention of Lloyd's name took Breland back. It will be exactly 50 years ago, on Halloween night, since Lloyd became the first African-American to play in the National Basketball Association by stepping onto the court for

Washington against the old Rochester Royals. The Washington franchise later folded, and Lloyd was signed by Biasone and Leo Ferris, the Syracuse general manager.

"Oh, yeah," Breland said softly. "I remember Earl."

To appreciate Lloyd's role, Breland said, you need to put yourself in that era. Lloyd played for Syracuse for six years in the 1950s, when the city's black population was confined to the old 15th Ward. "He lived in a boarding house on Fayette Street," Breland said, "because he really couldn't live anyplace else."

Lloyd, 72, now retired in Tennessee, is a soft-spoken guy with an easy sense of humor. He has fond memories of Syracuse, particularly the tight friendships he forged with his teammates, but he also can't forget the reality of the times. He would try to rent a place in "white" neighborhoods, only to arrive and find those homes had somehow become filled.

"Syracuse wasn't different than any other city," Lloyd said. "Still, I couldn't leave the 15th Ward and rent an apartment. That happened, man. That's just the way it was."

So he stayed on East Fayette Street, and he played pickup ball with neighborhood kids, and he spent many nights at the old Embassy Restaurant, a black nightclub that attracted national jazz acts.

Breland was 19 or 20, a Syracuse University underclassman and a budding star for the SU basketball team. He felt free to approach Lloyd at the Embassy. Lloyd became Breland's hero and his friend.

"I was fatherless, one of eight children," said Breland, a retired Syracuse school administrator. His life was changed by his good fortune in finding solid mentors. There was Ike Harrison at the Dunbar Center, a counselor who warned young Breland not to make basketball his only goal. There was Vinnie Cohen, Breland's roommate at SU, who'd stay up late every night, studying.

And then there was Lloyd, whose simple presence was a reminder of every kid's potential, a man of color who had made it in the NBA. "It was inspirational," Breland said. Basketball was taking off in the community, already eclipsing baseball as the city game of choice. Breland grew up playing pickup ball at Wilson Park on McBride Street, where the game carried that sense of release and celebration.

"I think some of that," said Breland, "was a function of Earl Lloyd."

As for Lloyd, he is both surprised and pleased that he'll be honored on the same day as Biasone, who died in 1992. He knows the story, how Biasone came to Syracuse as an Italian immigrant, how he credited the old Blodgett Vocational High School with transforming him, how the founder of the Nats always went for the underdog. "I think Danny may have been a little more sensitive than some others," Lloyd said.

That foresight helped put Biasone in the Hall of Fame, and it makes the tribute to Lloyd especially appropriate. The committee announced Wednesday that Dave Bing, a former SU great, will make the actual presentation. Lloyd, then working for the Detroit Pistons, scouted Bing when he played for SU, and they became close friends after Bing signed with Detroit.

Breland has a vision for the best way to honor Lloyd. He would love to see it done Nov. 29 in a city school, maybe Blodgett, a place that meant so much for Biasone and basketball. Breland dreams of a gymnasium filled with Syracuse schoolchildren, many needing some perspective on what's changed in 50 years, many—like Breland—growing up without a dad.

It's their turn, Breland figures, to be inspired by Earl Lloyd.

"Basketball Credentials Score Two"
April 11, 2003

Earl Lloyd, a key player in the Syracuse basketball championship, keeps asking himself if this whole week is just a dream.

"My feet aren't even on the ground," Lloyd said Thursday, and then he spoke with passion about great fans in Syracuse, and how they'd come out in the snow to watch him play.

Lloyd was a starting forward, but not for the Orangemen. He played with the Syracuse Nationals, who won the National Basketball Association title in 1955. Last week, on the day before Lloyd's 75th birthday, the phone rang at his Tennessee home. He found out that he'd been named to the Naismith Memorial Basketball Hall of Fame in Springfield, Mass.

The hall flew him and the other inductees to New Orleans for the Final Four. It was a nice way of closing the circle. Lloyd, a representative of the only Syracuse team to reign over the NBA, was an honored guest in the Superdome when Syracuse University beat Kansas for its first NCAA men's championship.

"Someone asked me who I was cheering for," Lloyd said, "and I just laughed."

He was pulling for SU, of course. Lloyd embodies our city's extraordinary basketball heritage. He is an African American who grew up in Virginia, in the segregated South. On Halloween night 1950, playing for a soon-to-be defunct franchise from Washington, D.C., he became the first black player to set foot on an NBA court. After that team dissolved, Lloyd was signed by Syracuse.

He spent the best years of his career with the Nats. In 1955, when Syracuse won it all, Lloyd and teammate Jim Tucker became the first blacks to play on an NBA championship team.

"We had a couple of shots at the championship and didn't make it [before we won], just like [SU]," Lloyd said. "And I'll tell you this: People talk about Jim [Boeheim] winning it because he's a good guy, or because he was due. But in the end, you win because you make the plays to win."

For the Orangemen, the big play was a Hakim Warrick block with a few seconds to go. For the Nats, it was a George King steal in the final minute that closed the door in a thrilling game with the Pistons of Fort Wayne.

Joined together, those two moments—48 years apart—turn into something new: Syracuse becomes one of the few cities in the nation that can boast of winning both an NCAA and an NBA basketball championship.

That NCAA title belongs to a Syracuse team composed primarily of African Americans, a direct link to such pioneers as Earl Lloyd.

"I'll represent a lot of people when I go in there," Lloyd said of the Hall of Fame. "I was born in 1928, in the heart of segregation. That was a desolate time. From the time you walked out of your house, there were no black police officers, no black postmen, no black bus drivers."

Throughout his life, his biggest fear was letting down all the people who believed in him, from childhood schoolteachers to administrators at West Virginia State University. For Lloyd, even at 75, his enshrinement is an affirmation of their faith.

It also speaks to the growing appreciation of the pivotal role played by Syracuse in basketball history. In 1954, the game-changing 24-second clock was used for the first time during a scrimmage at the Blodgett School, on Oswego Street. Danny Biasone and Leo Ferris, the men who ran the Nats, pushed for the clock and other NBA innovations.

The city itself is gradually waking up to the potential of that heritage, only enhanced by these heroics at SU.

The Erie Canal Museum on Erie Boulevard East is opening an exhibit dedicated to the Nats and the shot clock. The NBA helped to finance a much-needed playground for the children at Blodgett, as a gesture of thanks toward the birthplace of the clock.

And talks continue about the best design and location for a downtown shot clock monument, first suggested by Dolph Schayes, another Syracuse Hall of

Famer. The simple monument will feature a shot clock that eternally counts down from 24.

"Syracuse was a special place," Lloyd said. "That town embraced me. I've had a couple of long talks this week with Dolph and Red Rocha, my teammates. At that time, with all the segregation and other crap going on around the country, Syracuse was the right mix for us, and that was reflected in the way we played."

Lloyd said he'd be happy to make another stop in this city, especially for a chance to meet with children in the schools. His visit would allow Carmelo Anthony and his fellow Orangemen to shake the hand of a man who broke down walls to let them play, a guy who understands what it means to win a big-time title for Syracuse.

"I'm still just kind of floating," Lloyd said of the Hall of Fame. "The magnitude of this whole thing is still sinking in."

In Central New York, after Monday, we know exactly what he means.

"SU Salute One Step Toward Fading Color Line"
February 25, 2005

As children, Donald "Peewee" Caldwell and his brother Danny had it figured out. This was almost 70 years ago, when Wilmeth Sidat-Singh was a football and basketball star at Syracuse University. He rented a room in the old 15th Ward, maybe one short city block away from Peewee's house.

Sidat-Singh was a hero to the Caldwell boys. Eventually, Danny and Peewee—who still carries that nickname because he was always at his older brother's side—worked out a routine. If they left for school a little early, just before 8 a.m., they could time it so they always bumped into Sidat-Singh.

Every morning, they received a smile from their idol, who must have realized the encounters were no accident. Peewee, 77, a retired postal clerk, said no one needed to tell the boys why a student-athlete of national prominence was unable to live in a college dormitory with his teammates.

"You learned very early," Peewee said, "the rules of the game."

Like Sidat-Singh, Peewee is African-American, raised in a segregated United States. In the unspoken way of Northern cities of that era, Syracuse maintained strict divisions by color. Blacks were not served at most premier restaurants and nightclubs. They couldn't get jobs at many factories. During Peewee's childhood, you didn't see a black cop or firefighter.

23. Donald "Peewee" Caldwell, a retired postal clerk in Syracuse, has a deep sense of the history of the city's African American community. When Earl Lloyd played for the old Nationals, the two men were neighbors who've remained close friends for many years. Caldwell, shown here in 2005, was the first African American to play for the Le Moyne College basketball team in Syracuse. (Photo by Frank Ordoñez, courtesy of the *Post-Standard*)

As for Wilmeth Sidat-Singh, Syracuse University made a point of calling him a "Hindu," because some opposing teams refused to play against him once they learned who he really was:

A black American, who came of age in Harlem.

Saturday, Peewee hopes to be in the Carrier Dome for halftime of the SU-Providence game, when an entire community finally embraces Sidat-Singh. The university plans to hang his jersey alongside those of other SU greats, a fitting tribute for an extraordinary alumnus who died young.

He was killed during World War II while on a training flight for the legendary Tuskegee Airmen, an all-black fighter squadron created because black pilots could not serve side by side with whites.

To Peewee, the ceremony means as much in the city as it does on campus. The color line prevented Sidat-Singh from living in the SU dorms. Instead, Peewee recalls, he rented a room from Ted Brown, executive director of the Dunbar Center.

After college, when Sidat-Singh was barred from competing in the National Football League, he played for a time with the Syracuse Reds, a local semipro basketball team. His home, during that time, remained the 15th Ward. City resident Ernie Powell, 90, remembers how Sidat-Singh would sometimes train in a gymnasium at the Bethany Baptist Church on East Washington Street.

Powell and Peewee came of age when blacks in Syracuse were all but forbidden to live or socialize outside that neighborhood. The only lasting benefit, Peewee said, was a kinship that transcended money and celebrity. Right through the 1950s, when famous black entertainers and athletes visited the city, they had trouble finding bars or restaurants that would take their money.

Peewee recalls how such jazz artists as Dizzy Gillespie would routinely perform at mainstream downtown theaters before ending up at the Embassy lounge in the 15th Ward—a jazz club where Gillespie could get a sandwich or a drink.

At the Embassy, Peewee struck up a lasting friendship with Earl Lloyd, the first black to set foot in a National Basketball Association game. Lloyd spent much of his career with the Syracuse Nationals of the NBA. He could only rent an apartment in the 15th Ward, where he met Peewee, who'd already become the first black to play basketball at Le Moyne College.

Two years ago, when Lloyd was inducted into basketball's Hall of Fame, his old friend from Syracuse was among a handful of special guests.

"I've been exposed," Peewee said, "to so many outstanding people."

That started, in his youth, with such men as Sidat-Singh. Peewee is pleased that SU Chancellor Nancy Cantor and other administrators had the grace to put together Saturday's ceremony, even if a triumphant moment will inevitably be intertwined with pain.

"You're so happy to see this progress, but it makes you remember all the doors that weren't open and the opportunities that weren't there for you," Peewee said. Thinking back to his childhood, he recalls fine black students who wound up sweeping streets. He recalls young people with dreams of being doctors who struggled to find medical schools willing to let them in.

Those defeats, Peewee said, were "built and hammered into you." Even now, he said, many elderly blacks carry an unshakable regret. They wonder secretly, looking back on their long lives, what they might have done if only given a fair chance.

In that way, they still wear Sidat-Singh's jersey on their backs.

"Baseball Saga Takes Twist Through Syracuse"
December 2, 2005

Vic Power died Tuesday of cancer in Puerto Rico. In 1951, four years after Jackie Robinson broke baseball's color line, Power was the first black man to spend a season with the Syracuse Chiefs, giving him a place in local history.

When he heard the news, Don "Peewee" Caldwell was not thinking about baseball. Peewee, 78, a retired Syracuse postal worker, was thinking about the old 15th Ward in the city, the places black residents were not allowed to go and the bonds they formed as a way of getting by.

He was thinking about a young woman he once nicknamed "Lottie the Body," an exotic dancer from Syracuse who became a risque legend across the United States.

Peewee thought of her because—as Lottie said this week—Power was her "very good friend."

She lives now in Detroit, but she got to know Power when he spent that season with the Chiefs. He would later play for 12 seasons in the Major Leagues, where he became known as one of the great fielding first basemen of his era.

In Syracuse, Power arrived with two other black ballplayers, Nino Escalera and Al Perry. They came here in Perry's convertible, driving all the way from spring training in Florida because the Chiefs did not want them traveling through segregated states with their white teammates.

That segregation hardly ended in this city, where the three men were not allowed to stay in "white" neighborhoods. "We lived in the colored section with a guy who owned a liquor store," said Escalera, speaking Thursday from his native Puerto Rico, where he was celebrating his 86th birthday.

The "guy" was Frank Ellis, a successful businessman, Peewee recalls. Even though Escalera and Power saw themselves as Puerto Ricans, in the U.S. they endured the same treatment as all blacks. In Syracuse, that meant they were essentially banned from living or socializing in most neighborhoods outside the 15th Ward.

The same rules went for any blacks who came through town, Peewee said. It went for great athletes and great entertainers. It is why a guy like Peewee could walk into a local tavern in the 1950s and end up talking with Bill Russell or Jim Brown.

It is also how Vic Power and Lottie Bristow Graves crossed each other's path.

Power soon found himself as the only black player on the Chiefs, after the team got rid of Escalera and Perry. "In those days, it was tough for the white guys to play with the colored guys," said Escalera, who later became the first black player with the Cincinnati Reds.

While Power batted .294 to lead the Chiefs, his style grated on some of his white teammates: He wasn't quiet, and he was a showman who loved to turn a routine catch into a sweeping, one-handed drama at first base.

"They didn't like him in the States because he spoke out," Lottie said. "At that time, there was so much prejudice."

She would leave the 15th Ward, her childhood home, to build a national reputation. Lottie learned the fabled Lindy Hop in Syracuse, a dance brought here by Herbert White, the man who invented it. And she began polishing her exotic dancing at a place called Andy's and some other clubs in Syracuse.

That's how she attracted the attention of "Goose" Tatum of the Harlem Globetrotters. He married her and brought her out into the world, where her dancing career lasted much longer than the marriage. "Lottie the Body" became so famous that comedian Redd Foxx sometimes raised her name in awe on the television show, "Sanford and Son."

Before all that, in Syracuse, she spent time with a lonely ballplayer named Vic Power. She laughed this week when asked if she ever dated him. She said he used to come around to see her at the Elks Club, and that what she remembers about him are "secret" and "intimate things."

But she can also close her eyes and "see him playing ball," a game she said he played in a distinct, beautiful way.

Power was often frustrated, Lottie said. He felt that he deserved to get called up by the New York Yankees, who owned his rights, and he thought he knew exactly why it didn't happen. But he never stopped laughing, Lottie said, despite the barriers he found at every level of his life.

Years later, when she was dancing at a club in Kansas City, Vic stopped in one night to watch her show. She knew him instantly by his smile, and he came backstage after she was done to recall the best and worst times in Syracuse.

"He was a fun, fun, fun type of guy," Lottie said. "He loved to laugh. He had a grin. He had a smile and he was a great first baseman, but [baseball management] said for him not to talk too much because they didn't want anyone to know how wonderful it was to be free."

Vic knew. So did Lottie. They displayed it in their work.

"Nats Family Loses One Great Friend and One Great Foe"
November 4, 2006

Al Cervi is 89 and forgets nothing. He learned over the phone this week about the death of George King, a guy he coached 50 years ago. In his Rochester home, Cervi let out his breath almost as if he had been punched.

In 1955, King made two clutch plays for Cervi, a basketball Hall of Famer, that gave the Syracuse Nationals their only National Basketball Association title. The Nats were tied with the Fort Wayne Pistons with 12 seconds left in the seventh game of the 1955 championship series when the Pistons fouled King, the Syracuse point guard, who later coached college ball at West Virginia and Purdue.

On the bench at the downtown War Memorial, Cervi cringed. "He was about a 70 percent [free-throw] shooter and I had my face down in my hands," Cervi remembered. "I said to myself, 'Dear God, make this work.'"

King made the shot. The Pistons brought the ball upcourt, where King left his own man to knock the ball loose. The game ended and the Nats lifted King into the air. For the first and only time, they were NBA champs.

"When I stole that ball and the buzzer sounded and the next thing I knew I was up on those shoulders, that feeling can't ever be matched," King told The Post-Standard in 1995. "No matter how or what or when, that can't ever be matched."

He died Oct. 5 while in hospice care in Florida, according to news reports.

King's passing at 78 was one of two October jolts for his surviving teammates. The other was the death of Red Auerbach, architect of the Boston Celtics dynasty. Auerbach's reign as Celtics coach began in the 1950s, when Boston's explosive rivalry with Syracuse sometimes erupted into fistfights.

Through 1955, the Nats were the more successful team. Everything changed when Auerbach pulled off a complicated deal to bring Bill Russell, the great center, to Boston. To get the rights to Russell from St. Louis, Auerbach gave up Ed Macauley and Cliff Hagan, a couple of fine players. It was a daring move, especially for the times. McCauley and Hagan were white. Russell, an African-American rookie, had yet to prove himself.

Based on that trade alone, Earl Lloyd will always admire Auerbach.

"Let me tell you something, to have the courage and wherewithal to trade a couple of guys like that, it was off the charts," said Lloyd, 78, a power forward on the championship Nats who in 1950 became the first black to play in an NBA game. "Red knew. He saw the game that was coming."

Lloyd and Cervi agreed that Russell reshaped the NBA as they knew it. "We called him the 'Giant Eraser,' because any defensive mistake [a teammate] made, he erased," Lloyd said. "When you're outside, and you have no fear of your man beating you to the basket, you can lunge and take chances and do anything you want, because you know who's there if they beat you to the hoop."

Those who say Auerbach won only because of Russell miss the obvious, Lloyd said: Auerbach anticipated Russell's greatness, and he took some risks to bring Russell to the Celtics, and the result was the NBA's greatest dynasty.

Dolph Schayes, another Hall of Famer on the Nats, said that as a player he never really knew Auerbach. Most of the Nats saw playing the Celtics as a mixture of vendetta and crusade. That intensity gradually drained away after Schayes retired. He often spoke with Auerbach at Hall of Fame inductions and other basketball affairs.

"I really liked the guy," said Schayes, 78. "He had a soft spot for the old-timers; when people would say the old guys wouldn't be able to play the game today, Red used to say, 'The guys from the '50s could still do very, very well.' He was always in our corner when it came to trying to get a few more bucks [for] retirees out of the NBA."

While Schayes, Lloyd and teammate Billy Kenville appreciate the enormity of Auerbach's passing, they are in mourning for King, a close friend from an extraordinary era. Schayes remembers how the Nats went on a tour of the Middle East after the championship season. Children in Egypt and other countries would crowd around, Schayes recalled, while King took a basketball and put it between his legs and around his shoulders and mystified them with other ballhandling tricks.

Naomi Schayes, Dolph's wife, said the players and their wives formed a lasting bond during the long Syracuse winters. "The guys on that team were all quality guys who made no money, loved to play and still remain friends 50 or 60 years later," said Kenville, 75, who lives in Binghamton.

What brought them back, beyond all else, was relentless competition—a quality that never stopped burning inside Cervi. Even when it comes to the life span of contemporaries, he still keeps score. Cervi has had some recent trouble with bleeding ulcers. When he saw Auerbach's obituary, and noticed his old adversary was also 89, Cervi called out to his wife:

"Dear God, Ruth, I almost went before Red."

At the peak of the Syracuse-Boston rivalry, Auerbach "hated us with a passion," Cervi said. The two teams banged hips and threw elbows, while both coaches clenched their fists and screamed at the referees. Cervi remembers every catcall, every punch thrown, every foul.

He remembers because that's the way he loved to play, and the sight of Auerbach—young or old—always rekindled that fire.

"In spite of everything," Cervi said, "I was very sorry to see him go."

"A View on the Matter of Teachers, Community"
March 9, 2007

Earl Lloyd doesn't normally get calls seeking his thoughts on educational theory. Still, he is a thoughtful guy with strong opinions on teachers and their role in the community, and I thought of Earl amid the growing hubbub in Syracuse about whether the school district should impose a residency requirement on newly hired teachers.

That suggestion was made this week by Common Councilor Pat Hogan. It was quickly endorsed by seven other council members, although that hardly brings it close to being embraced by the district, especially since fewer than three of every 10 teachers in Syracuse, on average, now live in the city.

Considering that my wife is a teacher in the city and my children attend city schools, this is one of those columns where I figured I'd better turn to a fresh voice. So I got Earl on the telephone Thursday, mainly because I've often heard him speak directly to this question when he reflects on the reasons for his own extraordinary success in life.

Earl is intimate with our city. He lived here in the 1950s, when he was with the old Syracuse Nationals of the National Basketball Association. It is particularly significant that he once made his home in Syracuse, due to the position he holds in history:

In 1950, Earl became the first African-American to play in an NBA game. In 1955, when the Nats won the league title, he was the first black starter on an NBA champion. Eventually, he was inducted into basketball's Hall of Fame.

Yet when Earl talks about his most influential role models, the conversation invariably comes back to teachers, not athletes. He was raised in Alexandria, Va., in what he describes as "the cradle of segregation." From kindergarten through his college graduation, he never had a white classmate, much less a white friend.

It was part of the suffocating restrictions of life in a segregated America: Earl could not walk on certain roads in Alexandria, or eat at "white" restaurants, or sit where he wanted to sit on the bus.

His teachers were in the same boat, which caused them to approach their jobs with tangible fervor. Earl said they were revered because of a truth often voiced by his parents: The only glimmer of hope for a better life came from the schools, and the gatekeepers to that better life were the teachers, who saw the progress of each child as progress for everyone.

"When people let you know they truly care about you, all you want to do is please them," Earl said. "And there wasn't a kid who went into those classrooms [during his childhood] who wasn't feeling that."

Roughly 60 years later, a significant percentage of American children of poverty still end up unemployed, dead or in prison. In Syracuse, many of those boys and girls—and their parents—live in places where the borders of their neighborhoods become an unseen fence.

Teacher residency rules, by themselves, would hardly solve that problem. And the reality is that most teachers already living in the city have settled in traditionally middle-class areas: Eastwood, Strathmore, the Valley, the University district, and so on.

Still, living in any Syracuse neighborhood is a quiet statement of belief, and there is an implicit commitment that grows on many of those who settle there. You quickly become aware of how living in the city can be rewarding and safe, and how the passionate involvement of each family helps to keep it that way.

Beyond that, in Syracuse, children from all neighborhoods end up together in diverse city schools, and any parents who happen to double as teachers are often seen in their "civilian" lives in the community—at school concerts, sports events and science fairs . . .

That matters to the children they teach, according to Earl.

"I'll tell you this," he said. "When you walked into a market with your mother, and you saw your teacher shopping in the aisle, your whole attitude changed."

Now, anyone with kids in the city schools knows plenty of extraordinary teachers who drive to Syracuse from suburban homes. And I have close friends—dedicated teachers and administrators—who leave their houses in the city every morning to educate boys and girls in the suburbs.

To that end, if enforcing residency by decree might only lead to court fights and ill will, would it not instead make sense to use incentives to attract more teachers to choose a life in Syracuse?

What if new teachers who decided on city life were given a notable salary incentive? What if Syracuse University or Le Moyne College offered significant tuition breaks for the children of new teachers who settled in the city? What if public officials and private businesses came up with other creative offerings that might cause teachers—or police officers or other public employees, for that matter—to think first about making their home in Syracuse?

Earl likes that approach, although he also gives a warning: He would prefer to believe many teachers would live in their "school community" simply because they want to be there. What he remembers of his own childhood, beyond all else, is the empathy and love of teachers whose children were his classmates and his friends.

"It's like this," Earl said. "If you walk into a restaurant, you feel a whole lot better if the people who work there are eating the food."

"He Gave a Voice to the 'Invisible'"
October 17, 2007

Author's note: Earl and "Emo" Henderson are old friends.

For years, Emmanuel Henderson wrote for nothing.

During the 1940s and 1950s, Henderson had a full-time factory job with General Motors. At night, he made extra money as a janitor. In his free time, as a labor of love, he wrote a regular column in Syracuse for The Progressive Herald, a weekly newspaper that shut down more than 50 years ago.

"Writing for the paper was a minor thing," says Henderson, now 88 and living in Lyncourt.

His wife, Muriel, does not agree. Neither do many of Henderson's graying contemporaries, men and women of color who lived in the old 15th Ward in Syracuse.

And neither does the Syracuse Press Club. Its members on Thursday will include Henderson's name in their newest additions to the "Wall of Distinction" in the John H. Mulroy Civic Center, a wall honoring important Central New York journalists.

"When I heard they were recognizing him, I was elated," said Manny Breland, 73, a pioneering black educator in the Syracuse city schools. "He was kind of like our Walter Winchell, writing about who was seen here or who was seen there, sometimes with people who weren't their wives.

"But he was also our quintessential early-on advocate whenever he saw things he thought were unjust. Folks used to get [The Progressive Herald] just to see what Emo said."

At the time when Henderson wrote his column, the major newspapers in Syracuse paid scant attention to the black community. There were no blacks on the editorial staffs of The Post-Standard or the old Herald-Journal. Asked if he ever applied to be a writer at those papers, Henderson offered an emphatic shout: "Hell, no!"

It was unthinkable, he said. He could not cross the color line.

"We were totally ignored by the [large] papers, unless it was something bad," said Marjory Wilkins, 78, a Syracuse woman who has known Henderson since childhood.

For decades, she said, the only newspaper that covered daily life in the 15th Ward was The Progressive Herald. It was owned by J. Luther Sylvahn, who also wrote opinion pieces on issues of importance to black families. His wife, Helen, added a regular society column based in the neighborhood.

To Henderson, the Sylvahns are the ones who should be on the Civic Center wall. Still, Breland and others remember how the most popular feature in the paper was "This'N'That," a gossipy, into-everyone's-business column written by one "Blair Henderson"—"Blair" being Emanuel's middle name.

"It was always what you read first," said Peggy Wood, 94.

While it is difficult to find copies of The Progressive Herald, Wilkins supplied one from 1952 with a vintage example of "This'N'That." In that column, Henderson railed against violent husbands "who go upside their old ladies' heads." He offered a bevy of intimate hints about neighborhood life, such as how "the best molder in Syracuse is engaged also, or should I say again."

Muriel recalls how her husband was equally willing to enrage his own neighbors. He used easily recognized initials when referring to main characters in a story such as this: A husband, walking into his house, startles his wife while she is dallying with another man. The man then jumps out a bedroom window. . . .

Stark naked, as Henderson pointed out.

Muriel, at home, handled the angry calls.

Most important, he focused regularly on racial injustice. In that 1952 column, he took on the Syracuse police for some loitering arrests he perceived as unfair.

"All we in this neck of the woods are asking for is an even break," wrote Henderson, who routinely used his column to attack acts of discrimination, such as white Syracusans who refused to accept rides from black cabdrivers.

His friends see the Press Club honor as well-deserved, even if it carries a touch of tragedy. His work stood out in an era in which blacks "were kind of invisible," in the words of an old friend, Don Caldwell, 80. Henderson was a skilled, hard-working columnist when career options for black writers were profoundly limited.

"You kind of wish we could have lived then with the opportunities we have now, if you understand what I mean," said Muriel, 87, who married her husband 68 years ago.

The couple's sense of two Americas goes back to Henderson's birth. He is not absolutely sure of when he was born, because he has never been able to locate a birth certificate. As a small child, through his mother, he came to a love of books. The library to this day remains a favorite stop.

Even so, Henderson cannot recall a single teacher in Syracuse who encouraged him to be a writer. Instead, after high school, he looked to the factories. He and Muriel married young and were soon raising small children. The only writing Henderson got a chance to do was when Sylvahn highlighted "This'N'That" in The Progressive Herald.

The paper closed in the late 1950s. The column was gone, too.

"Am I angry about it?" Henderson said. "I'm angry at all times."

In reality, he displays more wistfulness than fury. Yet if he never got the chance to be famous as a writer, his columns still managed to provide a sense of place for readers too often made to feel as if they did not exist.

Those were his earnings, even as he worked for nothing.

"He is very special," said Marjory Wilkins. "I always looked up to him. I think most people did."

"Haven for a Hall of Famer"
February 13, 2008

An old water tower rises above West Virginia State University. It has been there to greet Earl Lloyd for as long as he remembers, going back to 1946, when a bus carried him toward the campus for the first time.

Seeing the tower, to him, always meant that he was safe.

Lloyd, 79, earned lasting fame in 1950 as the first black man to play in a National Basketball Association game. He retains powerful memories of Syracuse, where he had some of his greatest moments in the sport. It was in Syracuse, in 1955, that he became the first black starter on an NBA championship team. It was in Syracuse, over six NBA seasons, that he established the reputation as a physical and effective power forward that would help to carry him into basketball's Hall of Fame.

Yet those moments were not the highlights of his basketball career. That was evident Saturday, when an emotional Lloyd waved to the crowd from the floor of West Virginia State's tiny gymnasium in Institute, W.Va. He was joined by two elderly teammates from one of the great college basketball programs of the 1940s.

"It was more than a team," said Bob Wilson Jr., 81, a center whose jersey was retired during the reunion. "It was a beacon of change for things that were happening, a beacon of hope. Our goal was to demonstrate to the world that we could compete in every way, and that's what we did."

Sixty years ago, the West Virginia State Yellow Jackets finished off a 23-0 season by conquering the field at the Colored Intercollegiate Athletic Association tournament in Washington D.C. Among the stars were Lloyd and Wilson, who would both play in the NBA. Black newspapers of the time crowned the Yellow Jackets as the kings of college basketball—or, more correctly, of black college basketball.

They had no chance to play the great "white" teams of their time.

The achievements of that squad and its opponents are in many ways forgotten. The school was all-black, a byproduct of the "separate but equal" segregation laws known as Jim Crow. The players had to travel by car, not by bus. They ate sandwiches and slept on gymnasium floors, because they were not welcome in "white" hotels or restaurants. There were no press releases, no publicists. Mainstream newspapers paid little attention to their exploits.

Basketball in America would soon be changed—if not defined—by black players and black culture. And those who remember West Virginia State describe the Yellow Jackets as pioneers.

Between 1948 and 1949, they won 32 consecutive games. Their intricate "figure eight offense" was a hallmark of their coach, Mark Cardwell. There were rumors that West Virginia State would be the first all-black school invited to the prestigious National Invitation Tournament, rumors that never came to pass. Bill Himmelman, a basketball historian, suspects that such all-white schools as Kentucky would never have played in the NIT against an all-black squad.

To Lloyd, Wilson and Frank Enty, the three members of the team at last weekend's 60th reunion, the championship cannot be separated from the larger mission of the campus. It was at West Virginia State, Lloyd said, that he gained the confidence to cope with the almost entirely white landscape of the NBA.

"This was and is," Lloyd said of the campus, "a magical place."

His NBA experience cannot compete with that. To him, above all else, college meant sanctuary. Lloyd was raised in Alexandria, Va., a city he calls "the cradle of segregation." Black children learned quickly what they could and could not do. They did not use public swimming pools. They did not go to the white movie theater. They did not walk down the streets of white neighborhoods.

They were all too familiar with tales of lynchings, beatings and racial violence. "The only place where you felt safe," Lloyd said, "was at school or at home."

Even as an adult in Syracuse, a city that provides Lloyd with many fond memories, he was not free from segregation. He was forced to live in a 15th Ward boarding house because blacks could not rent homes beyond that neighborhood. In the 1950s, plenty of clubs and restaurants in Central New York still maintained a color line, he said.

Those realities underline Lloyd's devotion to West Virginia State. He went there on the advice of his high school coach, who had played for the Yellow Jackets under biology professor A. P. Hamblin, the coach who also mentored Cardwell. Through those connections, Lloyd arrived with an understanding of the school's complex offensive system.

Within the borders of campus, he experienced real freedom for the first time in his life. His nickname became "Moonfixer," given to him by upperclassmen who expected this freshman to make the moon come out, even on a cloudy night.

He was also embraced by the faculty and the student body, which created a sense of gratitude that Lloyd, Enty and Wilson say they honor to this day. "You did your schoolwork and you played ball real hard because you didn't want to let any of those people down," Lloyd said.

Betty Cardwell Spencer, the daughter of Lloyd's coach, still works at the campus. Her father, she said, taught his players a philosophy that emphasized the mission of the school: "Hold your head up and be dignified," Spencer said. "Never act the way some people expect you to act."

Lloyd made the same points Friday, when he showed up at a practice for this year's Yellow Jacket basketball team. The players gathered around him in a circle on the court. Many stared at Lloyd's Hall of Fame ring as he spoke of how they should respect their coach, even when they disagree.

He told them the college years are irreplaceable, a fleeting time in their life that will never come again. "Don't waltz," said Lloyd, who also spoke of why every young person ought to vote.

"People have died—been hung or burned or thrown in lakes—for you to have that right," Lloyd told the players, most of whom were black. "People died for you and you're not going to exercise that right?"

The players rushed forward to shake his hand and pose for photographs. He spoke to them, one by one, as they left practice. Then he stepped back, in that tiny gym, and he remembered.

The 1947 season began with a struggle. West Virginia State outlasted Tuskegee University in overtime, 63-61. Lloyd can still describe a Tuskegee buzzer shot that bounced off the back of the rim and barely missed. After the game, relieved at getting away with a win, the Yellow Jackets were hardly dreaming of an undefeated season.

No one would come that close to them again. Game after game, West Virginia State blew other teams away. They traveled in two DeSotos, a pair of automobiles bought by the athletic program after Cardwell had a run-in with a West Virginia bus driver who insisted the players go to the back of the bus.

The driver won, Lloyd recalled, but Cardwell refused to allow his team to be humiliated again. The players would pack into the cars for long road trips. Bobby Vaughan, 80, a conference historian who coached at Elizabeth City State University in North Carolina, recalls how schools would roll out cots "so players could sleep on the gym floor or in the lockerroom."

The coaches knew of every black hot dog stand on the circuit. Restrooms were often tobacco fields, Vaughan said, since gas station toilets were not open to blacks.

The conditions were harsh, but change was in the air. Jackie Robinson had just shattered the Major League baseball color line with the Brooklyn Dodgers. Enty said his teammates would gather around a radio in their dormitory to listen as Robinson played in the 1947 World Series.

Early voices for justice were being heard on campus. Paul Robeson, in the late 1940s, visited West Virginia State. A. P. Randolph, a black labor activist, came to nearby Charleston, where he called on American blacks to boycott the military until it was fully integrated. Eleanor Roosevelt, the widow of the president and a champion of human rights, spoke at the college at least twice during that time.

The basketball team made its own statement in 1949, the season following the national championship. Cardwell and his players were invited on a tour of the West Coast, where they became the first all-black college to play against white teams in San Francisco's Cow Palace. In West Virginia, when the players left, a crowd of 2,000 came to the train station to see them off.

While the 32-game winning streak ended with a 66-52 loss to St. Mary's, one of three defeats on the tour, the Yellow Jackets proved to themselves that they were able to compete with a 57-44 win over Santa Clara.

Even Lloyd's big breakthrough, his selection in the ninth round of the 1950 NBA draft by the old Washington Capitols, was linked to West Virginia State. The CIAA championships were played every year in the Uline Arena, home court for the Capitols, which made it easy for the team's executives to notice Lloyd.

Almost 60 years later, West Virginia State is a very different school. The enrollment of 2,800 is now about 90 percent white. The men's basketball program is winning again, although it plays in the same tiny gymnasium in Fleming Hall. That makes Lloyd wonder why his alma mater, after all these years, has not received government support for a new court.

As for the members of the national championship team, basketball Coach Bryan Poore promises to keep bringing them back. Today's players, he said, need to know their history. To Lloyd, Wilson and Enty, that tradition is defined by what they remember when they see the water tower.

In an era when the law itself was meant to break them down, they learned how integrity and diligence became their only chance. It was a lesson invoked by every teacher and coach in that cluster of red-brick buildings, a lesson that Lloyd seeks to pass down to children at risk today.

"People ask me what I did in basketball that was most important," he said. "I tell them about this place. Because if you take this out of the equation, there's nothing else."

Earl Lloyd's Career, Playoff, and Coaching Statistics (NBA)

Career statistics[a]	G	FG-M	FT-M	PTS	PPG	REB	A
1950–51 Washington	7	16-35	11-13	43	6.1	47	11
1952–53 Syracuse	64	156-453	160-231	472	7.4	444	64
1953–54 Syracuse	72	249-666	156-209	654	9.1	529	115
1954–55 Syracuse	72	286-784	159-212	731	10.2	553	151
1955–56 Syracuse	72	213-636	186-241	612	8.5	492	116
1956–57 Syracuse	72	256-687	134-179	646	9.0	435	114
1957–58 Syracuse	61	119-359	79-106	317	5.2	287	60
1958–59 Detroit	72	234-670	137-182	605	8.4	500	90
1959–60 Detroit	68	237-665	128-160	602	8.9	322	89
Career totals	560	1,766-4,955	1,150-1,533	4,682	8.4	3,609	810
		.356	.750				

Playoff statistics[a]	G	FG-M	FT-M	PTS	PPG	REB	A
1952–53 Syracuse	2	4-17	7-10	15	7.5	9	5
1953–54 Syracuse	10	25-73	17-26	67	6.7	57	20
1954–55 Syracuse	11	44-122	39-52	127	11.5	89	35
1955–56 Syracuse	8	26-81	13-14	65	8.1	43	7
1956–57 Syracuse	5	12-30	7-11	31	6.2	21	5
1957–58 Syracuse	3	5-14	0-0	10	3.3	8	0
1958–59 Detroit	3	9-28	8-8	26	8.7	18	7
1959–60 Detroit	2	6-24	5-8	17	8.5	9	3
Playoff totals	44	131-389	96-129	358	8.1	254	82
		.337	.744				

Coaching statistics[b]	W	L	PCT
1971–72 Detroit	20	50	.286
1972–73 Detroit	2	5	.286
Coaching totals	22	55	.286

Source: Statistics courtesy of the National Basketball Association.

[a]G = games; FG-M = field goals made; FT-M = free throws made; PTS = points; PPG = points per game; REB = rebounds; A = assists

[b]W = won; L = lost; PCT = percentage

Index